THE AMAZING WORLD OF
Orchids

The Royal Horticultural Society

THE AMAZING WORLD OF Orchids

A practical guide to selection and cultivation

WILMA AND BRIAN RITTERSHAUSEN

photography by Linda Burgess

ALHAMBRA EDITIONS

This edition first published in 2009 by
Alhambra Editions
Alhambra House
27-31 Charing Cross Road
London WC2H 0LS
www.quadrille.co.uk

EDITORIAL DIRECTOR Jane O'Shea
ART DIRECTOR Helen Lewis
EDITOR Simon Davis
DESIGNER Katherine Case
SPECIAL PHOTOGRAPHY Linda Burgess
PRODUCTION DIRECTOR Vincent Smith
PRODUCTION CONTROLLER Denise Stone

Cataloguing-in-Publication Data: a catalogue record for this book is available from the British Library.

ISBN 978 184400 793 6

Printed and bound in China

Published in association with the Royal Horticultural Society
80 Vincent Square, London SW1P 2PE
www.rhs.org.uk

CONTENTS

A world of orchids

Orchids hold many secrets. Their origins are steeped in mystery and the mists of time, and, as very little fossil evidence has been discovered, no one can be sure when they first appeared on earth. While their exact origins may remain unknown, both the evolution and structure of orchids are much clearer. Orchids have adapted and modified their features to take advantage of every environment on earth. Opportunists, they are equally at home in forests, grasslands and swamps, as in deserts and other drought-ridden areas.

In recent years there have been many exciting advances in the world of gene technology which have resulted in a number of orchids being reclassified as more information about their relationships becomes available. The world authority for the taxonomy of orchids is based at the Royal Botanic Gardens, Kew. It is the Kew World Monocot Checklist that has been our reference for this book. For hybrids the Royal Horticultural Society in London produce the *International Register of Orchid Hybrids*. These have been our references to ensure that, at this time, the latest accepted names have been used in the book.

ABOVE
With its fairytale blooms,
Dendrobium *Ekapol can,*
like so many varieties, be
traced back to a very few
species. The most dominant,
D.phalaenopsis, *was*
discovered on one of Captain
Cook's expeditions to
Australia.

The evolution of orchids

Orchids are thought to have originated during the early Cretaceous period, some 120 million years ago, when the continents we know today were breaking away from the original great land mass of Pangaea. At this time the first orchids already existed, possibly occupying an area which is now Malaysia. As the tectonic plates of this super-continent slowly drifted apart, so the orchids moved with them and became dispersed around the world.

One of the orchids which was once widespread across this ancient land mass was *Vanilla*, whose pods are used for flavouring. The original position of this genus on Pangaea can be related directly to where vanillas are found growing naturally today. From their central location they were carried across the oceans towards their present homes in Africa, South America to the west and Malaysia to the east. *Dendrobium* is another huge orchid genus which also has an extensive range and which diversified into one of the largest genera, containing nearly 1,000 species found throughout China, India, South-East Asia, Malaysia, Australia and New Zealand. A further genus of great travellers, the slipper orchids (*Cypripedium*) became circumborial, having circled the globe to straddle North America, extending into Europe to Russia, China and Japan, but not appearing anywhere south of the equator. The related *Paphiopedilum* slipper orchids spread down from China and India to South-East Asia and into Indonesia, while their relatives, *Phragmipedium*, continued in a similar march through Central America to beyond the Panama Isthmus and into the Andes of South America.

While the most adaptable orchids have expanded over a huge area, others which are much more specialized have hardly moved at all and their habitat is more localized. This is true of *Cattleya*, found only in South and Central America, which may indicate that these and related genera are younger than the more primitive vanillas, or that they were insufficiently widespread to be carried on more than one piece of the disintegrating super-continent, Pangaea.

Ten thousand years ago, the last ice age covered much of the northern hemisphere, but as the ice receded and the frozen earth warmed up, abundant life returned to colonize the land again. In evolutionary terms this period is very short, so the flora in this part of the globe is limited both in numbers and in diversity of species. Britain, for example, is home to only about 55 native orchid species compared to the tens of thousands which arise in the world's tropical rainforests which were not affected by the ice age to the same extent, and where evolution continued unhindered for hundreds of thousands of years.

Today, orchids colonize every part of the world except the arctic regions, where conditions are too severe. Everywhere else they have adapted and continued to evolve into the huge, multiformed and highly successful family of plants called Orchidaceae. They represent the largest plant family with the greatest diversity of flora on earth. Estimates suggest the number of naturally occurring species is over 25,000, with new species being discovered even today. The species are divided into approximately 750 separate genera, according to their main characteristics. The most diverse accommodate hundreds of different species (for example, *Bulbophyllum* and *Dendrobium*), while others contain from a few (such as *Ada* and *Brassavola*) to a single specimen (*Amesiella philippinensis*).

The structure of terrestrial orchids

Orchids may be either terrestrial or epiphytic in their growth. The terrestrial orchids grow in the ground, mostly in forest or woodland leaf litter and in grassland over a wide area but they also occur in almost any terrain, from deserts (*Eulophia petersii*) to semi-aquatic

BELOW
The dramatic-looking slipper orchid, **Phragmipedium longifolium**, *is usually terrestrial, growing in the leaf litter of forests from Costa Rica to Colombia.*

(*Hammarbya palugosa*). In arctic Russia species of *Cypripedium* flourish under the snow, their flowers appearing as the snow recedes in spring. Even more extraordinary are the two Australian species of *Rhizanthella*, only discovered in 1928 by a farmer ploughing his fields. These orchids are completely subterranean, growing and flowering entirely under the ground.

Terrestrial orchids appear in great numbers in tropical and temperate regions where they cover hillsides in huge swathes. These plants are threatened by the advance of agriculture, the use of herbicides and other man-related activities such as mining and afforestation. Up until now they have been rarely cultivated, due to legisation protecting their environment where it still exists, as well as to the difficulty of raising them from seed and keeping them in good condition. Some of these problems have recently been overcome, however, and enthusiasts are starting to find that terrestrial species can now be cultivated with a measure of success.

Terrestrial orchids produce underground tubers – usually two, sometimes one – or tuberous roots from which arise an erect stem, leafed at the base and terminating in the inflorescence. The leaves vary from long and narrow to broad and short and from one to many. Like all orchids, terrestrials are perennial herbs: they have a growing season followed by a dormant period. Once the annual growth dies down for the winter, only the flowering stem with seed capsules remains visible. Wild populations can fluctuate greatly from year to year. Where hundreds or thousands of flowering plants may be observed in one season, the following year their numbers may be a fraction of this.

The structure of epiphytic orchids

Epiphytic orchids grow on the trunks, branches and extremities of trees. They are not parasitic but have adopted trees as their home in order to secure a space closer to the light and fresh air in areas where competition from other ground-dwelling plants would be intense. In this way they have evolved an existence whereby only the toughest of plants can survive. They absorb moisture from the air through their aerial roots, without harming the tree upon which their life depends. The tree is only in danger from the largest of these epiphytes (*Grammatophyllum speciosum*) which grow on the huge ironwood trees in the Philippines. Reaching up to five metres (16 feet) long and completely encircling the trunk, their weight can in time bring down the tree, though the orchid will continue to grow on the ground for many more years while the tree decays. The life expectancy of most orchids is directly related to the tree's lifespan, which could be hundreds of years. Some epiphytes (*Stanhopea*, for example) produce their flowers on pendent spikes suspended below the branch upon which they grow. Here, should the tree

fall, the plants will continue to grow but are unable to produce their flowers: the flowering spikes bury themselves in the leaf litter and die. During its lifetime the orchid plant progresses forward along the branch as an advancing chain of new growths leave behind the older, dead and decayed pseudobulbs (see page 12).

Epiphytic orchids are more diverse than the terrestrials in their plant structure, but more particularly in their flowers. With few exceptions, orchids are pollinated by insects and their methods of attracting the right one from among these masses are fascinating and complex. With millions to choose from, each orchid has gone to extraordinary lengths to ensure that, usually, just one specific insect will be attracted to its flowers. This is why they have become so highly specialized, with huge variations between the species. While the more popular and widely cultivated orchids are easily recognized and the flower parts apparent, for every well-known type there are hundreds of lesser-known orchids, whose flower parts almost defy description, stretching the imagination and testing our powers of identification to the limit.

Found mainly in tropical regions, epiphytic orchids grow wherever it is sufficiently warm for their aerial way of life without the danger of their exposed roots becoming frozen. Their extreme southern location is in the temperate rainforests of Australia and New Zealand. Their main habitats, and the regions where they have attained their evolutionary zenith, are the equatorial forests. Here, the most flamboyant forms appear to know no bounds, their exotic beauty being unequalled in the orchid kingdom. It was these tropical epiphytic

orchids which first inspired the early growers and set the horticultural world alight. But epiphytic species are in danger of extinction too, some seriously, owing to the destruction of the tropical rainforests. This is a further threat to orchids whose populations were gravely depleted during the nineteenth century through over-collecting. In many cases the survival of these plants rests with botanical gardens, national parks and nature reserves, where different orchids can be bred to establish healthy cultivated populations all around the world.

Epiphytic orchids make one of two types of growth, sympodial or monopodial. The majority of them are sympodial, producing new growth from a node at the base of the mature pseudobulb; this develops and flowers usually within one season. The plant progresses forward in this way until, over several years, a string of interdependent growths is built up, each attached to the previous one by a rhizome. Further progress is achieved when two growths are produced from one, the plant spreading out in the manner of an iris, eventually doubling its size. But orchids have no permanent structures. The roots and leaves may live for one season only, as is the case with pleiones or calanthes, or for several years as in both the cymbidiums and the odontoglossums.

Most sympodial orchids produce pseudobulbs, which are not true bulbs but swollen stems used for water storage. They are the longest surviving part of the plant and usually remain for five or six years. Inside they resemble a tuber rather than the embryo leaf bracts of a true bulb such as a daffodil. These pseudobulbs vary greatly in their size and shape: they may be round, conical or elongated into long stems or canes, depending on the genus. During their lifetime they support the

FROM LEFT TO RIGHT

Coelogyne
The plumped, leafed pseudobulbs of this sympodial orchid contain food reserves for the plant. New growths start from the base of the previous one. Roots also develop from the latest pseudobulb but both leaves and roots will be outlived by the pseudobulbs which can remain for several years after these have died. Old leafless pseudobulbs, termed back bulbs, can be used for propagation (see page 216).

Cattleya
*The tall, thin pseudobulbs of this **Cattleya** hybrid each support a single semi-rigid leaf, identifying it as one of the unifoliate group. Cattleyas have an apical flowering habit, with long or short flower spikes produced from the top of the latest pseudobulb in season.*

Cymbidium
Cymbidiums produce the most leaves of all the popular orchid types. Their hard pseudobulbs are round and sheathed with the bases of the leaves which are long and narrow, gracefully arching along their length. The flower spike is produced from the base of the leading pseudobulb. Extremely free-flowering, cymbidiums can produce up to six flower spikes on an adult plant in a year.

Odontocidium
*All orchids in the **Odontoglossum** alliance are distinguished by their green, cone-shaped pseudobulbs which typically support a pair of basal leaves and a pair of long, narrow apical leaves. The flower spikes, which appear from inside the lower leaf at its base, may be long or short, and from few to many-flowered.*

Dendrobium

Sympodial orchids, dendrobiums get confused with monopodial types because of their tall, cane-like pseudobulbs which carry leaves along their entire length. New canes are produced from the base of older ones until a sizeable plant is built up. While the newer canes will bloom in their season, older canes eventually become leafless and can be propagated.

Stanhopea

The sympodial stanhopeas produce oval ribbed pseudobulbs each with a single broad leaf, but the flower spikes appear from the base of the pseudobulbs and grow downwards. Their tip burrows through compost to emerge beneath the plant, where the blooms open. For this reason they are grown in open slatted baskets.

Paphiopedilum

Slipper orchids are sympodial orchids which do not produce pseudobulbs. Their several-leafed growths are produced one in front of the other in succession over the years. As the older growths die away, newer ones take on the main supportive role. Each new growth blooms once, as it matures, when the flower spike emerges from between the central fleshy leaves.

Vanda

The monopodial vandas produce their semi-rigid leaves in pairs from an ever-extending stem or rhizome. Their thick aerial roots, produced from the base and higher up the stem, are fleshy and easily snapped. Grown in open baskets, vandas have little need of compost, provided they are grown in a humid atmosphere where the roots can absorb moisture. Flower spikes appear between the leaves once or twice a year.

orchid's leaves and roots until the leaves are shed or the roots die naturally. Once a pseudobulb becomes leafless, it is known as a back bulb and, while no longer actively supporting its own leaves and roots, it assumes a supporting role for the plant, maintaining the younger pseudobulbs with the last of its reserves. Eventually, these old pseudobulbs die, by which time several newer ones will have taken their place, perpetuating the orchid which remains strong and which continues to grow and to flower.

Each pseudobulb may support from one to a dozen or more leaves, depending on the genus. The leaves of sympodial orchids are as varied as the pseudobulbs and may be long and narrow or short and thickened. Cattleyas produce a single broad, leathery leaf above elongated pseudobulbs, while odontoglossums and miltoniopsis produce one or two apex leaves from the top of the pseudobulbs, with two shorter basal leaves. Cymbidiums have long, narrow leaves, up to ten of them emerging from broad sheaths which enclose the pseudobulb. Some dendrobiums have very tall, cane-like pseudobulbs with short, rounded leaves along their length. Other sympodial orchids, including paphiopedilums and related genera, have no pseudobulbs but instead produce sturdy growths, each with several leaves which may be short and rounded or long and narrow, with many examples in between. The roots of sympodial orchids may be either thin and fibrous, or thick and fleshy. Plants in pots form dense rootballs which, when unwound, can reach up to a metre (3 feet) long.

Monopodial orchids exhibit a different type of growth. In these plants, which include *Vanda, Phalaenopsis* and many other less well-

RIGHT

*In the monopodial growth of **Phalaenopsis**, the thick, fleshy leaves grow from a single rhizome which extends upward as new leaves are made at the apex. Older leaves are shed naturally at about the rate new ones are made, so an adult plant rarely consists of more than five leaves. Flower spikes appear from the stem between the leaves.*

known orchids, a single upward-growing rhizome produces leaves from the apex in alternate succession, until a fan of leaves is built up. *Phalaenopsis* are short and stout, developing one new leaf at a time, at a rate of one or two a year. The older leaves at the base are shed naturally from time to time so that the plant maintains an average of four to five leaves at any stage. Some vandas, on the other hand, continue to extend vertically, adding pairs of alternate leaves until they are up to a metre (3 feet) or more high. As the older leaves drop away, a bare stem is left from where new aerial roots will grow. These roots, produced above the rim of the container, are thick and brittle and can become very long.

The flower structure

Orchid flowers are produced on various types of inflorescence, loosely termed 'spikes', although more correctly the flowers are held on racemes. These may be basal (produced from the base of the plant, as in *Cymbidium*, *Odontoglossum* and *Lycaste*), apical (where the spike comes from the apex of the pseudobulb, as in *Cattleya*), or axillary (as in *Vanda* and *Phalaenopsis* where the spikes come from the stem opposite the base of the leaf). Some orchids carry a single bloom while others can support as many as a hundred or so. The most popular orchids in cultivation typically have from six to a dozen flowers on a spike which may be naturally arching, upright or pendent or can be trained accordingly. The flowers may either appear on side branches or be produced directly from the main stem.

Orchid flowers show the widest diversity of any plant family and this is where they differ most obviously from all other flora. With so many differences, one wonders how they can all be orchids. It is their complex structure and seemingly limitless adaptations which have given rise to this infinite variation on a single theme. All orchid flowers, whether colossal or minute, whether European terrestrials or tropical epiphytes, conform to one basic pattern. Each flower consists of an outer whorl and an inner whorl. The outer whorl contains three sepals which resemble the petals in substance and colour and contribute to the flower's size and overall design.

Structure of the orchid flower (*cymbidium*)

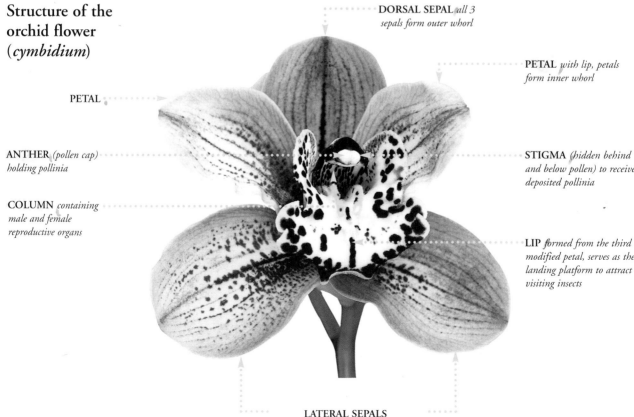

DORSAL SEPAL *all 3 sepals form outer whorl*

PETAL *with lip, petals form inner whorl*

PETAL

ANTHER *(pollen cap) holding pollinia*

STIGMA *(hidden behind and below pollen) to receive deposited pollinia*

COLUMN *containing male and female reproductive organs*

LIP *formed from the third modified petal, serves as the landing platform to attract visiting insects*

LATERAL SEPALS

The inner whorl consists of two lateral petals, with a third petal between them which is greatly modified to form the lip, or labellum.

The lip's function is to act like a flag, signalling to a passing pollinator. An orchid's lip makes an ideal landing platform for the visiting insect, attracted by its coloured markings, distinct from the rest of the flower and known as the honey guide. Orchid flowers take elaborate steps to ensure that the insect they wish to attract alights in exactly the right spot to accomplish pollination. Indeed, it is the specific pollinator which defines the size and shape of the lip. Where this has become diminutive the flower may attract a certain midge or small fly. Where the lip has become almost inconspicuous it is compensated for by the enlargement or fusion of the sepals or petals. Some masdevallias produce exaggerated and highly coloured sepals, while the petals are reduced to the size of the lip, hardly visible at the centre of the flower.

The lips of various orchids show great ingenuity and while some are highly complex structures, others are relatively simple in their design, but all achieve the same aim. Some are rigidly fixed, as in odontoglossums, and others have a moveable hinge, found in cymbidiums, where the bee has to be of the right size to push its way into the flower. The lip of many anguloas is constructed so that it will rock back and forth at the slightest movement. Lip sizes also vary in relation to the size of the flower and reach their maximum in cattleyas and sobralias, where they become very flamboyant and are the most attractive part of the flower. In oncidiums also the lip is greatly exaggerated, while the petals and sepals are reduced and partially hidden by the lip. In *Euanthe sanderiana* and its hybrids it is the

large, broad sepals which are most highly patterned, while the lip is much reduced. In some species of *Bulbophyllum* and *Pleurothallis*, the lip has become almost non-existent and a strong odour replaces it as the main attracting agent. Some lips can be hairy or have hairy adornments, such as that of *Bulbophyllum barbigerum* which resembles a carefully constructed fishing fly and which moves erratically at the slightest movement.

In the genus *Coryanthes* the lip has become even more strangely adapted – it hangs, bucket-shaped, beneath the flower. Upon opening, the flower exudes a liquid which drips into the lip cavity and when the flower is visited by small bees they become extremely agitated, nibbling at the rim of the lip. Some fall or are pushed in, where they swim to a single opening which allows them to escape, with pollinia (pollen masses) attached, to the next flower. Pollinating insects are enticed, trapped and occasionally rewarded by the orchid they visit, but never intentionally killed, and no orchids ingest insects. Paphiopedilums and related orchids are commonly called slipper orchids because their lip is modified into a pouch, which bees are encouraged to enter. Orchids are not carnivorous and the insect is always released, through a specific exit, after unintentionally delivering and collecting pollen.

In the majority of orchids the lip is positioned at the bottom of the flower but in a few species, like *Prosthecea cochleata* and *P. radiata*, the lip is uppermost. In the bud stage of most orchids the lip is above, but as the flower opens, the stem twists through 180 degrees until the lip is in what we think of as its normal position. Called resupination, this occurs in all popular genera.

At the centre of the orchid flower is a single, finger-like structure called the column, which contains both male and female reproductive organs. At the end of the column is the anther, or pollen cap and beneath this easily dislodged cover you will find the pollen. Unlike other plants, whose pollen is loose grains, the orchid pollen is held in tightly compacted masses. There are usually two, but sometimes more, little packets called pollinia; golden yellow, they are attached to a sticky disc by two threads. Having solid pollen ensures that none is wasted, unlike wind-blown pollen which requires vast quantities to be produced because so much is lost to the air. Behind and below the pollen is located the stigma, a small hollow with a sticky surface to which pollen attaches when the pollen-bearing insect lands on the flower and, attracted by the honey guide, forces its way into the centre looking for nectar. Upon leaving, that flower's pollen becomes stuck fast and is carried by the insect on to the next flower.

Sometimes the insect is attracted by a particular orchid's ingenious use of mimicry. A number of the European species of *Ophrys*

have highly developed methods of affecting this. Their lips appear very lifelike, resembling the body of the bee, fly or spider they wish to attract. Scent also plays a part in this deception, with the orchid mimicking the scent of the female. In one species, for example, even the orchid's flowering time is crucial, with its bee-like flower opening just three weeks before the female bees emerge, at a time when the males are already on the wing. Searching for the elusive mate, the male bee believes he has found the real thing and attempts copulation. This interaction between flower and insect is a finely tuned relationship, where in some cases both are dependent on each other for their continued existence, however in this instance the bee does not receive a reward.

FROM FAR LEFT TO RIGHT
These examples demonstrate the extraordinary diversity of orchid flowers. The small lip of **Anguloa uniflora** *is hinged to rock back and forth; in* **Masdevallia** *Whiskers the fused, long-tailed sepals dominate, while the insignificant petals and lip are partially hidden inside the flower; the flared* **Oncidium flexuosum** *lip is grossly exaggerated and very decorative, with the reduced petals and sepals inconspicuous behind it;* **Miltonia clowesii** *has star-shaped flowers, with pointed lateral petals and a fiddle-shaped lip; in the slipper orchids (shown here,* **Paphiopedilum** *Pinocchio) the lip is modified into a pouch which traps the pollinating insect, with the two lateral petals fused behind it.*

There are other quite startling examples of this dependency among the tropical orchids, in which rewards are offered. Madagascar is the home of *Angraecum sesquipedale*, sometimes called the comet orchid owing to the extra-long spur which is a tube-like extension at the back of the lip. Its specific name means 'a foot and a half', referring to the length of this spur, at the bottom of which is tempting nectar. When this orchid was discovered in the mid-nineteenth century, Charles Darwin predicted that an as-yet unknown species of hawk moth with a proboscis the length of the spur must exist, otherwise the orchid would never be pollinated. It was much later, and after his death, that this moth with a long enough proboscis was eventually found – it was subsequently named *Xanthopan morgani praedicta*, after Darwin's prediction.

Fragrance also plays an important part in attracting pollinators to orchid flowers. Many of the epiphytic species are deliciously scented, a good enough reason on its own to cultivate them. *Oncidium ornithorhynchum*, *Coelogyne ochracea*, *Maxillaria picta* and *Prosthecea radiata* are a few of the best examples. However, these orchids are not fragrant for 24 hours a day. Depending on when the pollinator is on the wing, some orchids are scented only at night, as with *Brassavola nodosa* and many species of *Angraecum*, which make use of night-flying moths. Others produce their scent earlier or later in the day, or only when the sun is shining. Scent also wanes as the flower ages. Not all fragrances are sweet; some orchids make use of carrion flies and smell of rotting meat; these strange plants with grotesque flowers are found among the bulbophyllums. While the strongest fragrance persists in the species, a number of primary hybrids retain some degree of scent, but most often in the complex hybrids all trace of scent is usually lost. Miltoniopsis and cattleyas are exceptions and the modern hybrids, many times removed from the original species, are still sweetly scented, making them even more desirable to the collector.

Most orchid flowers are bisexual, containing both male and female organs, but separate male and female flowers are occasionally produced. In catasetums and cycnoches these differ notably in size and colour, leading the early taxonomists to believe they were dealing with two separate species.

Phragmipedium *Eric Young illustrates the different flower structure of slipper orchids in the manner in which their lip is modified into a pouch. They also have two anthers, one on either side of the rostellum (equivalent to the column) and therefore two exits for the pollinating insect.*

Seed and mycorrhiza

When an orchid has been fertilized by a pollinating insect, the stem immediately behind the flower, which contains the ovaries, begins to swell. Eventually, after a period of a few to nine months, it develops into a pear- or oval-shaped seed capsule, by which time the flower itself has dried and shrivelled up. The seed capsule may contain anything up to a million minute seeds which, collectively, are a beautiful pale yellow and resemble fine sawdust. Studied under a microscope, it can be seen that each seed is encased in what appears to be a string bag.

In the wild the seed is wind-blown. As the capsule ripens it splits along longitudinal seams to release the seed a little at a time, over a period of days, to be carried away on the air currents. Of the tens of thousands of seeds released, only a very small amount (less than one per cent) will germinate and grow. The extremely low germination rate is a result of the seeds' dependency on mycorrhiza, a micro-fungus which in turn needs the seed in order to survive. This dependency is not unique to orchids, for many plants and trees have a symbiotic relationship with their own mycorrhiza. Only those orchid seeds lucky enough to land where their specific mycorrhiza already exists have a chance of surviving. This is likely to be an area where the orchid is already established, cohabiting with the fungus. Once endowed, the mycorrhiza infects the seed and the two develop their relationship, each dependent on the other for their continued existence. In time the mycorrhiza is confined to the orchid's roots and the surrounding area. In cultivation the seed is harvested before coming into contact with the air and is kept sterile until it is sown straight into glass containers on a medium that contains all the basic nutrients for germination and growth.

Species and hybrids

An orchid species has two parts to its Latin name, the first being the generic or genus name, for example *Cymbidium*. The second element is the specific epithet which distinguishes one species from another, as in *lowianum*. A species is a wild, naturally occurring plant with usually little or no difference between individuals, called clones. Occasionally, however, sufficient variation does appear, with distinct flower colouration, size or markings to justify a varietal name being given to

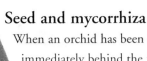

ABOVE
*Once an orchid flower has been pollinated, it collapses and dies, while the stem behind the flower swells to form the seed capsule, seen here on **Prosthecea cochleata**. It takes several months for the capsules to ripen before they split along vertical ridges, with the seed trickling out to be carried away on the wind. Note the shrivelled flower remains below the capsules.*

the specific clone, such as *Cymbidium lowianum* var. *concolor*. So there exist species and their variations which can, over millions of years, evolve into separate species in their own right and many orchids are still actively evolving today.

Where separate populations of related species exist in the wild in close proximity, sharing the same pollinator, there arises the opportunity for cross-pollination between them, thus creating a natural hybrid. However, these occurrences are quite unusual in nature and the resulting hybrids will not generally go on to breed further. Termed mules, they appear to be incapable of further reproduction.

Hybrids are more usually the result of a grower, or breeder, deliberately crossing two different species together; the first cross produces a primary hybrid. Further generations of breeding can achieve intergeneric hybrids, where specimens of related genera are crossed together. In this way orchids have achieved a far greater degree of hybridizing than any other plant family, greatly extending the range of plants and in most instances providing enhanced colour, size and general appeal. In the last 150 years, since the first hybrids were produced, over 100,000 orchid hybrids have been officially registered, with about another 3,000 new ones being added each year.

ABOVE
Rhynchostele bictoniensis was an early species to be introduced into cultivation. (1835) and first flowered at Bicton in Devon, England.

BELOW
With its deep pink lip and dark mottled leaves **Rhynchostele** *Violetta von Holm 'Wilma' is a compact, free-flowering hybrid of the species* **R.bictoniensis** *and* **R.rossii**.

Diverse habitats

Experts in survival, orchids are the most durable and toughest of all flowering plants. They have exploited the most unlikely situations, spreading away from the warmer environs of the equator to within the edges of the harsh arctic regions of Russia and Alaska in the north and south, to the extremities of the great land masses of South America and Australia. Their adaptability is legendary. For example, in the tropical regions stretching from Africa and Madagascar to South America and the West Indies there exists a curious orchid which scrambles through the tree branches to climb high into the canopy on long vine-like stems. Here its leaves are thick and fleshy, its roots only occasionally extending down to the ground. This is the vanilla (*V. pompona*) whose pods give the flavouring for culinary use. Other species of vanilla, however, such as *V. humboldtii*, grow in desert conditions, creeping along at ground level where their leaves are reduced to tiny leaf bracts with short and stunted roots, relying instead upon the fleshy stems to retain sufficient moisture for survival. The vanilla was originally grown by the Aztecs of South America for its flavouring and introduced into Europe by the Spanish conquistador Cortes, in the sixteenth century. Today vanilla is the only orchid grown as a commercial crop for its fruits, the dried seedpods from which vanilla essence is obtained. The flowers are mostly large and showy, yellow or green, but they are individually very short-lived, often flowering for less than 24 hours. In cultivation vanillas are shy-flowerers until they become extremely large and given full sun, when flowering becomes almost continuous.

Along the coast and estuaries of Venezuela and spreading through the

LEFT
Vanilla pompona is a native of tropical South America where it inhabits forested areas, scrambling vine-like through the trees.

CENTRE
A native of only very cold climates, the endemic terrestrial orchid Cypripedium guttatum can be found growing from Alaska to North East Asia.

RIGHT
Since the discovery of orchids over 200 years ago, plant hunters have searched mountains and forests all over the world to bring back new species for collectors. Coelogyne cristata was found growing on the trunks and thick branches of trees high in the mountains of Nepal.

islands of the West Indies are vast mangrove swamps, a muddy saltwater environment that would seem an unlikely place to find orchids, but here, too, one notable species has made its home. Growing on the mangrove trees and shrubs just above the high-water mark lives the showy *Caulathron bicornatum*. The plant is also unusual because it has hollow pseudobulbs which, as they mature, develop small splits at the base, encouraging a species of fire-ant to enter and produce their colony inside. This association clearly provides some form of protection for both orchid and insect but it would also have made collecting the plants extremely hazardous. The plant is in cultivation, however, and has been used sparingly in hybridization, its showy white flowers adding grace to its progeny. Other salt-tolerant orchids can be found off the coasts of Thailand and Malaysia where sheer-sided limestone cliffs and sea stacks rise vertically from the water. Here, in the most inaccessible of places, a slipper orchid, *Paphiopedilum bellatulum*, clings with scant roots to the rock faces, apparently unaffected by the constant drenchings of saltwater.

In temperate climates terrestrial orchids (such as species of *Epipactis*) grow happily in sand dunes close to the sea. And Alaska and Russia can boast tundra-growing orchids, little plants which grow and flower in the short summer season while the ground is free from snow (species of *Cypripedium* and *Planthera*). While these are some of the more extreme habitats occupied by orchids, the majority are found in less dramatic situations. Every continent and island has its own indigenous orchid populations but, as we have seen, it is the equatorial regions that hold the main treasure trove of orchid species.

Phalaenopsis has become today's top indoor flowering orchid. The almost constant temperature of a centrally heated home suits these warm-growing orchids well, providing conditions close to those they enjoy in the wild.

The home environment

Orchids that exist in extreme conditions around the world are not generally those found in cultivation. Their specialist culture would not produce the rewards expected by enthusiasts, who prefer to grow orchids with the largest, showiest and most colourful blooms. These species of orchid and the many hybrids raised from them can, for the purpose of growing them at home, be divided into three main cultural categories, determined by the environment in which they grow in the wild. The main categories of cool-, intermediate- and warm-growing orchids are more fully explored later in the book.

Cool-growing orchids include those that live at high altitudes in the wild such as *Cymbidium,* *Odontoglossum* and some dendrobiums, as well as *Prosthecea* and *Coelogyne*. The first three are readily available in a multitude of hybrids encompassing the entire colour range, while the smaller-growing prostheceas and some coelogynes are ideal where space is limited. They will all grow well indoors provided they are not exposed to excesses of temperature such as will occur in a sunroom or conservatory which can easily overheat in summer. Likewise, these orchids will not thrive in an area left unheated during the winter. Choose a well-lit part of a living room which is not directly in the sun; it needs to be warm by day and cool at night. Intermediate orchids include the fabulous tropical American cattleyas, as well as warmer-growing slipper orchids and *Miltoniopsis*. Grow the exotic cattleyas in a warm room with good light, where some background heating can be left on overnight in winter. Slipper orchids and miltoniopsis need a slightly shadier position to protect them from direct sun.

The warmest-growing of all the popular varieties are *Phalaenopsis*. These moth orchids originate from the hotter environments found at lower elevations in the forested tropics of Asia and Malaysia. With their wide, fleshy leaves and their tendency to make aerial roots, they need a warm but shady position where they can be kept constantly moist. They also require warm night-time temperatures but should not be placed too close to a heat source, which would dehydrate them.

Having selected a position for each plant which corresponds most closely to its natural environment, you can set up a small growing area consisting of a humidity tray filled with pebbles. Maintain moisture by keeping the pebbles damp, watering the orchids regularly and spraying lightly when possible. Provided their basic cultural needs are met, more specialized treatment can be given for individual orchid groups (see Orchid Families, pages 24–57).

Orchid families

The most popular genera contain a bewitching selection of colourful themes and shapes of startling beauty. Consider the allure of the fashionable long-blooming *Phalaenopsis*, or the sheer abundance of bloom of the magnificent cymbidiums, whose towering flowering spikes dominate the right situation for months, mostly in the winter when little else flowers. Amongst the *Odontoglossum* types daintiness combines with intricate lacy patterns in a multitude of colours of almost unlimited availability. For flamboyance and fragrance the light-loving cattleyas and their allies are unsurpassed – while those with an eye for a challenge should consider growing the irresistible, winter flowering, hard-caned dendrobiums, or the exotic, warmth-loving vandas with their exquisite (and exclusive) indigo-blue colouring.

Cymbidiums

It is often said that cymbidiums owe their popularity not to the fact that they are easy to grow, but because they are difficult to kill. When grown well, however, they are among the most rewarding and desirable orchids for growers the world over. One of the loveliest aspects of cymbidiums is their ability to bloom throughout the dull winter months when little else flowers.

Cymbidiums produce leafy, evergreen plants which stand about 60cm (2ft) tall, and over 90cm (3ft) in bloom. Their hardened pseudobulbs each carry eight long, narrow leaves. The flowers, which may be from 5–10cm (2–4in) across, depending on the type, are carried on a spike that grows from the base of the newest pseudobulb. Flower spikes appear in the latter part of the year, once the summer growing is completed, and extend throughout the winter until buds become visible and open in their season. Their flowering season now continues almost throughout the year as new hybrids are raised to cover most months.

The flowers, which will last for up to ten weeks, are of an almost waxy texture, the well-rounded sepals and petals of equal size. The lip, which is the third, modified petal, is of similar size and kaleidoscopically patterned in a thousand different ways individual to each specific plant. The fantastic colour range for cymbidiums extends from pristine white to shades of pink and red, encompassing brown and cream, and also includes spring greens

and fresh-faced yellows. Every colour except blue can be found in this one genus. Depending on the hybrid, a single flower spike can support from six to 15 long-lasting blooms, shown at their best when the spike is allowed to arch gracefully and naturally. A large plant which has been grown on to specimen size can provide an astonishing display, with up to six flower spikes in bloom in a single season.

Cultivation

Growing cymbidiums is not difficult, providing a few basic rules are followed, and there is no reason why the plants should not continue to grow for many years. It is quite common to find varieties still existing in established collections raised in the 1920s or 1930s. To understand what a cymbidium requires by way of care, we must look at how the original species grow in the wild. The majority of the species used for hybridizing come from the Himalayas, where the plants grow as epiphytes in the forks of large trees. As old trees die and crash to the ground the orchids can adapt and re-establish themselves on rocky outcrops or in well-drained soil, where they continue to live for many years. In the high altitude of the mountains they receive dappled sun on bright sunny days with high light levels, while at night there is a considerable temperature drop, often to below freezing. Because of the elevation, the plants can tolerate low temperatures, which is not always the case in cultivation.

In many parts of the world, such as California, parts of Australia, northern New Zealand and many African countries, cymbidiums will grow outdoors either as garden plants or under shade houses. But in

ABOVE
An attractive clone of the popular, fragrant hybrid Summer Pearl, 'Sonya' is a miniature variety. The hybrid comes in a range of colours and flowers into the summer months.

LEFT
The brushed petals and sepals on the lovely Valley Splash 'Awesome' give an unusual bi-coloured flower reminiscent of a watercolour in its delicacy. Up to 12 waxy blooms are produced on an upright flower spike taller than the foliage; they will last for 8–10 weeks during the winter. See page 66 for full entry.

growing roots to penetrate right through to the bottom of the pot. If you are concerned, about six weeks after repotting, carefully tap one plant out of its pot and inspect the roots: if they remain circling the top of the compost and not growing down through it, the compost is unsuitable and you will have to repot the cymbidium again, using a less dense compost. After repotting, keep the plant moist to encourage it to make plenty of new roots. The roots follow the new growth which continues well into early summer, by which time flower spikes will be showing. These early spring and summer months are critical in initiating the flower spikes.

Once the spikes become visible, they will shoot up like a bullet at the base of the newest pseudobulb until they reach their maximum height. As soon as they appear, insert a thin bamboo cane into the compost close to the spike but away from the rim of the pot where most of the new roots will be circling; tie the flower spike to the cane as it grows. If left unsupported, the spike may grow out at right angles, making the flowers difficult to display as well as putting them in danger of being accidentally knocked off. You cannot stake unsupported spikes later because the flowers will be badly placed on the stem and will not right themselves once open.

During the latter months of the year in the northern hemisphere the day length shortens and light levels drop. Artificial heating will be needed to maintain a healthy temperature, which should drop to not less than 10°C (50°F) at night, rising by at least 3–4°C (10°F) during the day. Where dull weather persists and sunshine becomes a rarity, buds may start to drop; this is the result of an imbalance between the temperature and the

Europe and cooler parts of America the ideal home for them is a high-roofed greenhouse or conservatory where they can enjoy plenty of light and fresh air which imitates their natural conditions. In the spring you can shade the greenhouse to reduce the heat and prevent scorching the foliage. Leave the shading in place until the end of summer, then remove it to give the plants full light in winter.

Repotting, when necessary, should be carried out in the spring. The compost (see page 200) needs to be well-draining and durable, and open enough to allow the fast amount of light getting to the plants. Keeping the plants too warm at night, as well as the other extreme of being too cold, often combined with dampness, will cause the buds to turn yellow and drop off. This usually occurs when the buds are on the point of opening and chemical changes are taking place within the unopened flower as colour pigmentation flows into the petals and sepals.

While little can be done to compensate for lack of sunshine, albeit filtered, the daytime temperature can be kept in balance with the humidity to provide the combination of factors which lead to good culture. Artificial lighting is not always a logical option within a greenhouse but it can be beneficial indoors. Cymbidiums growing well in the greenhouse may be brought indoors during their flowering period to be enjoyed to the full. To prevent the risk of bud-drop, do not move the plants until the flowers are all open on the spray.

If you have acquired a *Cymbidium* as a pot plant and wish to grow it on to flower the next year, do not be surprised if the blooms appear in a different season. Your plant may have been reared to bloom at a specific date, like Easter or Christmas, and the varied and less exact conditions you can provide may well result in a different growing time. Reflowering will in any case only be achieved with patience and attention to detail. If left indoors, where the light is poor compared with outside, and the temperature almost constant, cymbidiums are unlikely to bloom again and their growth will be soft, with limp foliage. For this reason they do not make good all-year-round house-plants.

To succeed with cymbidiums, take the plants outside once the last frosts have become heavy dews and find a shady position. Gradually move them into a more exposed, sunny place until they are sufficiently hardened off to remain where they receive morning or late afternoon sun, but are shaded from the midday sun which would scorch their leaves. Avoid putting the plants in a north-facing position where the light will be little better than indoors. The base of trees with a light canopy of foliage, where dappled sun will reach the plants during the day as the sun passes overhead, would be an ideal position, closely resembling a natural habitat. The cooler nights outside, compared with indoors, will encourage tougher growth capable of initiating the flower spikes near the end of summer. When night temperatures begin to drop, bring the plants inside before the danger of a frost becomes a reality.

While cymbidiums are out of doors, pay close attention to their watering needs. Exposed to sun and wind, they can dry out quickly, but during long rainy spells they may need to be covered with polythene sheeting or moved under shelter to stop them becoming saturated at the roots. Add feed at every second watering. When you bring your plant back indoors, clean the leaves and remove any dead bracts from around the pseudobulbs. Check it and the compost over for insect pests, placing the plant in a bucket of water for half an hour to purge it of unwanted visitors. Indoors, find a well-lit position, preferably in a conservatory until the nights become too cold, finally bringing it into a room once the buds open, where it can remain until the first flowers fade. Cut off spent flower spikes about 2.5cm (1in) from the base with a sharp knife or secateurs. Cymbidiums, unless otherwise stated, should be given a position in light shade in summer and full light in winter, reducing their watering in winter.

ABOVE
The pretty colour combinations seen in **Cymbidium** *Mini Splash 'Fantasy' are the result of breeding programmes which go back to the early years of hybridizing at the beginning of the twentieth century.*

Odontoglossum Alliance

Odontoglossums and the numerous natural and specially bred genera related to them are highly decorative and easy to grow. Early Victorian growers referred to odontoglossums as the 'queen of orchids' because of their petite, dainty blooms which appeared so feminine. Once they had found favour, hybridizing proceeded at a great pace, involving related genera including *Cochlioda, Miltonia, Miltoniopsis, Oncidium* and many more, all of which combine to make up the *Odontoglossum* alliance, the resulting man-made hybrids being known as intergenerics. Many species originally classified as odontoglossums have since been botanically separated into genera of their own and the whole group has now been revised.

Odontoglossums are evergreen plants producing green pseudobulbs and two pairs of flexible, mid-green leaves. The flower spikes come from the base of the leading pseudobulb and may carry from five to literally a hundred or more exquisite, long-lasting blooms, produced at almost any time of year. The modern, highly complex hybrids within this extensive group are varied and excitingly different from any other group of orchids. Odontoglossums may be self-coloured or patterned and decorated in a multitude of designs. With the exception of green there is no colour not represented, with mauves and purples

bordering on blue being predominant, alongside gorgeous reds and yellows as well as white. This exceptionally broad spectrum of colour is the result of extensive breeding over the last 200 years.

Cultivation

Although there exists an abundance of dazzling hybrids to tempt you into growing, few of the species remain in the wild. This is a direct result of mass over-collecting which continued unabated until 1915. While the species are rare and classed as specialist collector's items, the very best *Odontoglossum* hybrids are mass-produced and available worldwide. Their cultivation is the same as for *Miltoniopsis* (see page 34), with watering all year round and a cool, shady position. The only exception is that they can be grown slightly cooler, at a minimum temperature of 10°C (50°F), with a general maximum of 24°C (75°F). The ideal pot size, unless otherwise stated, is 10cm (4in).

ABOVE
The individual blooms of this intergeneric hybrid, **Odonchlopsis** *Bert White x* **Odontocidium** *Goldrausen are a deep fiery red. The colour extends evenly across the petals and over the lip, with a little white flecking towards the bloom's centre.*

LEFT
Odontioda *Aviewood illustrates the poetic beauty of a pure white flower, with the occasional dot and adornment on the lip.*

RIGHT
The exquisitely patterned **Odontioda** *hybrid,* **Odontioda** *Quedlinburg, shows the influence of its* **Odontoglossum** *parentage in its primrose-yellow flowers which are overlaid with colourful red markings.*

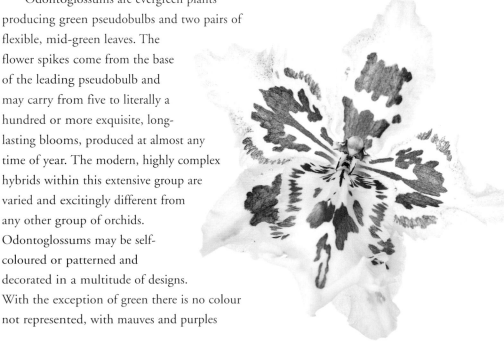

Oncidiums

This is by far the largest genus of the three from the *Odontoglossum* alliance included here, comprising more species than the miltoniopsis and odontoglossums together. They are also far more varied but, surprisingly, not grown in such large numbers. These epiphytic plants are widely distributed throughout South America, as far as northern Mexico and down through Florida, and including the various islands of the West Indies.

Extremely variable in their growth, oncidiums display several distinct habits. There are those with green pseudobulbs resembling those of odontoglossums, but producing very lengthy flowering spikes, their flowers small and curiously shaped and the dominating lip well-defined and decorative. There is a prominence of bright, golden yellows and soft autumnal shades of brown and tan. Another well-known group are the mule-ear oncidiums, whose stiff, erect leaves are mostly solitary, with diminutive, hardly recognizable pseudobulbs. They produce tall flower spikes with bright sunshine-yellow flowers arranged in a spreading effect at the top of the stem. This group can vary from a few centimetres tall to giants with 30cm (12in) leaves and flower spikes reaching to over a metre (3–4 feet); they will grow in slightly warmer conditions than those with true pseudobulbs and need good light to flower well.

The finest hybrids among the oncidiums have come from Mexican species, such as *O. tigrinum* and *O. incurvum*; these are the pseudobulbous kinds which, when crossed with the Andean odontoglossums, produce the vibrant colours and finely chiselled flowers of the odontocidiums. They are vigorous, stout plants resembling a large *Odontoglossum*, the flower spikes tall and sometimes branching and the boldly coloured flowers highly varnished in combinations of rich mahogany or plum, bright yellow or tiger brown, distinguished by large yellow lips. These intergeneric hybrids are the best of the group to grow. Sturdy, stunningly beautiful and tolerant of cool to warmer conditions, they are at home indoors or in a greenhouse, where they can be given good light and plenty of water, with feeding throughout the year. In temperate climates they can spend the summer outdoors, the harder growth produced by this treatment ensuring a breathtaking display of flowers each year.

Cultivation

Oncidiums, like most of the complex hybrids within the *Odontoglossum* alliance grow in a nine- or ten-month cycle. This is the time the plant takes to produce one pseudobulb, after which it blooms and the next seasonal growth starts. Repotting, when necessary, should therefore be done when there is a new growth just showing. By avoiding the coldest and the hottest months of the year, you can repot or 'drop on' a plant during spring or autumn, provided it is not in flower. Repotting immediately after flowering, before the plant has started to grow, can cause pseudobulbs to shrivel, so delay it until you see the growth developing well, but before new roots are produced. These fine roots, white with green growing tips, can become extensive within the pot, so the compost should be open and well-draining: a fine grade of bark chippings suits them well. Plants with tall flower spikes need

RIGHT
With its compact short foliage and multitude of fragrant, delicate flowers **Oncidium** *Twinkle is a delightful primary hybrid. The flower spikes are packed with dozens of flowers that can be counted in the hundreds on a large plant.*

supporting from the time they emerge to when they are in advanced bud; use a thin cane to hold the spike upright to the base of the buds, when it can be allowed to arch naturally.

Where a minimum winter night temperature of 10°C (50°F) is maintained, most plants in the *Odontoglossum* alliance can be grown together. Plenty of fresh air, together with cool summer days, are important to these high-altitude orchids. The daytime temperature should not rise above 24°C (75°F), and this can be controlled more easily in the home than in the greenhouse. Continual damping down and sufficient shading, combined with open ventilators day and night, should keep the greenhouse cool. In warmer parts of the world a shade cloth construction which allows fresh air in from all sides is a good idea. For all odontoglossums, think shade! Continue watering all year round and grow in a 10cm (4in) pot, unless otherwise stated.

Miltoniopsis

These beautiful 'pansy orchids', loved for their huge, flat blooms with fanciful pansy faces, were once classified as odontoglossums before being split from them botanically. They are similar in appearance and share similar habitats, which range through the high Andes in Colombia to Peru and Ecuador. The most favoured species come from Colombia, producing glistening flowers in shades of pastel pink and white. Those from elsewhere were divided off yet again into the genus *Miltonia*; these lack the large appealing flowers but produce smaller, elegantly refined blooms on longer sprays.

Miltoniopsis have two main flowering seasons, which peak in early summer and again in autumn. They are extremely free-flowering, regularly producing two or three flower spikes on one pseudobulb. There can be up to six blooms on a spray, their highlight being the gloriously radiant decoration on the lip known as the mask. This is always in stark contrast to the rest of the flower, where colours sweep through dazzling white, primrose-yellow, pretty shell-pinks until the deepest of rich reds emerge, close on purple and mauve. These wondrously coloured flowers also carry a sweet honey fragrance which, on a warm sunny day in the greenhouse, fills the air from morning to night. While the odontoglossums have long been prized as cut-flower orchids, the flowers of miltoniopsis do not last when cut from the plant. Blooms which will remain on the plant for five to six weeks in perfection, will droop immediately once they have been cut.

Cultivation

Miltoniopsis make wonderful display orchids for both indoor and greenhouse culture. Their foliage is of a softer texture than that of the odontoglossums, and a lighter green; excessive amounts of light cause them to turn pale and insipid, so an indoor environment is ideal. Create a cool, shady area where there is some humidity from a tray of wet pebbles and keep the plants evenly moist at the roots throughout the year. Continue watering all year and feed the plants lightly during the summer months. Avoid overwatering but do not allow pseudobulbs to shrivel from being too dry, or this will cause corrugation of the young leaves. The delicate foliage of miltoniopsis is easily marked and the plants should not be sprayed

RIGHT
Miltoniopsis St Helier 'Plum' is one of the Jersey-bred orchids whose bold, decorative designs include the butterfly-shaped mask at the centre of the flower. See page 84 for full entry.

overhead; it is better to keep the leaves, and especially the flowers, dry at all times. Never overpot the plants, as this can lead to their being overwatered, so grow them in as small a pot as possible (usually 10cm/4in) and repot annually, or at 18-month intervals. *Miltoniopsis* can be 'dropped on' into a slightly larger pot for several years without disturbing the existing rootball. Only after a long period of time, when the compost at the centre of the rootball has deteriorated and there are dead roots in the middle, need they be repotted into fresh compost and have their fine, extensive roots thinned out.

While miltoniopsis are regarded as cool-growing orchids, they will exist happily in slightly warmer conditions. Dropping the temperature to the coolest in the range, as is possible with cymbidiums, will not be good for these orchids. Prolonged cold and damp can be detrimental, so it is better to keep them on the slightly warmer side, which is why most indoor conditions suit them well. Unless otherwise stated in the individual entries (see pages 84–93), the ideal temperature range for all miltoniopsis is a minimum of 12°C (54°F) and a maximum of 25°C (77°F). They prefer to be kept in a growing position away from direct sun.

ABOVE
Miltonia clowesii *is a species from Central America belonging to a small genus once included in* **Odontoglossum**, *but now separated from it. The plants are related, however, and some interbreeding has given further variety to hybrids within the* **Miltonia** *genus. See page 90 for full entry.*

Coelogynes and Prosthecheas

These charming orchids make ideal indoor plants, where they quickly adjust to the drier atmosphere, produce a long-lasting flowering display and have a superb fragrance. These distinct genera are horticulturally grouped together because their cultural requirements are (apart from a range of warmer-growing coelogynes) identical, and their growth exhibits similarities of size and adaptability. Following recent research, a large number of orchids previously categorised as encyclias have now been moved to *Prosthechea*.

The cool-growing coelogynes range from China down to India, and as far south as New Guinea, including many of the islands which exist between the two mainlands. Others have extended their natural range to Borneo and Malaysia and need more warmth. Prosthecheas are from the New World, covering parts of South America but mostly found in Mexico and the West Indies; they are all cool growing.

All coelogynes and prosthecheas are compact, evergreen plants with a fine rooting system, mostly grown in pots. Their pseudobulbs may be rounded, oval or, as in some prosthecheas, long and thin; they produce a pair of leaves from the top of the pseudobulb where, with a few exceptions, the flower spike emerges. Among coelogynes the pseudobulbs are often crowded, growing close together and clump-forming on a large plant. Among the intermediate coelogynes are some superb evergreen plants producing large, oval to cone-shaped pseudobulbs topped by two wide,

ribbed leaves up to 60cm (24in) long.

Flowering extends from early spring through summer, their flowers enchanting, often sweetly fragrant and long-lasting. Colouring is predominantly white or creamy white, with yellow, light brown, green and orange-red also represented. Some prosthecheas hold their flowers with the lip at the top, all coelogynes with the lip at the bottom.

There are very few hybrids available within these two genera and it is the species, which propagate freely, that are grown. Many have been in cultivation from the time of their original importation over 100 years ago.

Cultivation

Both coelogynes and prosthecheas have a resting period of several weeks in winter, before any new growth is seen in the spring; start watering again once the new growth extends from the base. In most coelogynes, the flower spike develops early, from within the centre of the young growth, to produce its spring blooms. Prosthecheas complete most of their growing before the flower spike emerges from between the top leaves, in early summer. Water them well during this time, keeping them evenly moist at the roots, and feeding lightly at every second or third watering.

Once they start to grow, coelogynes often shrivel as the new growths take their nourishment from the older pseudobulbs before new roots develop, but within a short time the pseudobulbs will fill out. Overhead spraying is also beneficial during growth.

Keep the plants well shaded in summer, gradually extending the amount of brightness until they are in full light for the winter. At the start of the inactive period, the plants should be supporting well-matured, plump

pseudobulbs storing enough water to take them through the dry rest. Water in winter only if some shrivelling starts; alternatively, spray the leaves to prevent dehydration.

A bark compost suits these orchids well, and while they can be grown in pots, they can also be accommodated in hanging baskets and left to grow on to specimen size if you have room. Where space is limited, keep them small by dividing about every three years. Unless otherwise stated, provide these orchids with a minimum temperature of 10°C (50°F) and a maximum of 30°C (85°F).

The warmer-loving coelogynes should be grown in the greenhouse, where there is enough headroom for their large leaves and where they will have a minimum temperature of 13°C (55°F). These orchids need plenty of water and feeding from spring through summer, with light shade overhead. Their new growths will take all season to develop and when the pseudobulbs have matured they can rest until new growth starts again.

Dendrobiums

Dendrobiums are an immense genus whose extremely wide geographic distribution extends throughout Asia as far north as China and through the whole mainland down to the islands of the Philippines, New Guinea and Borneo, as well as most of Australia and New Zealand's North Island. With such vast distribution there have evolved many distinct types adapted to almost every climate, some of which have become very popular with enthusiasts and have produced many colourful hybrids. Others, more obscure, are of less general interest but still rewarding to grow.

Dendrobium nobile types

Dendrobium nobile is a pretty species originating from the Himalayas, which has been in great demand for over 100 years. Today it has been superseded by a multitude of superior hybrids, available in a bewildering array of colours, produced by crossing *D. nobile* with other related species to bring together the finest qualities of each.

These plants produce tall, jointed pseudobulbs, loosely termed canes, giving rise to their common name of 'bamboo orchids'. The pseudobulbs, or canes, grow to 30cm (12in) or more tall, with short, oval, flexible leaves in alternate pairs along their length. Flower nodes are produced from the side of the canes opposite each leaf base and develop short stems, each with usually two flowers. The decorative flowers are characteristically rounded, with the sepals and petals cupped around a circular lip. The colours combine white, yellow, pinks and mauves, the flowers often tipped with brighter shades, enhanced by an eye-catching disc at the centre. Crimped edges give them an attractive frilly look.

Cultivation

This group of dendrobiums has a fast summer growing period, followed by an extended winter rest. Their cultivation is quite challenging but the rewards are great as the decorative flowers can cover the entire plant for weeks in spring. Early in the year these orchids start their new growths from the base of the main plant as the embryo buds along the canes become active in response to the lengthening days and warmer temperatures. They need little water until the buds are more developed, but from then on, step up watering and add feed to every other watering, so the plants never dry out until the end of the growing season. New growths develop quickly, followed by an abundance of new roots, while at the same time the buds progress fast and the flowers open together along the canes. The flowering canes (pseudobulbs) are usually those of the previous year, although older canes can produce flowers from previously undeveloped nodes. After flowering, place the plants in good light, but not direct sun, for the summer. In warm climates they may spend the summer outdoors in the same way as cymbidiums, giving more light and air to produce a harder growth which will bloom all the better in spring. Plants grown in a greenhouse should remain where they are, as they will benefit from relatively high summer daytime temperatures of up to 30°C (85°F). Balance the humidity and spray the leaves regularly, keeping plants moist at the roots.

ABOVE
Prima Donna is a **Dendrobium nobile**-*type hybrid with regal blooms. The Indian species has had a dramatic effect on the flowers raised from it, well-rounded in shape and heightened in colouring.*

These fast-growing orchids will complete their season's growth within five months, whereas other orchids may take up to twice as long. By summer's end the long canes will have matured, a single terminal leaf signalling their completion. Yellowish canes indicate that enough light has reached the plants to ripen them prior to winter. From now on, keep in full light and reduce water and feed until, by the end of the year, the plants are dry. They can rest in this state until new activity heralds the start of the growing season, during which the pseudobulbs should remain fat – shrivelling indicates they are not having enough water, but a good soak in a bucket of water for an hour should put this right. Shrivelling during the winter rest may indicate inadequate watering the previous summer, but if too much water has to be given during the winter, the plant will not produce flowers. If watering is started too early in spring, before the buds are definable, the nodes will become adventitious growths instead of flowers. This natural propagation provides extra plants in time, but cannot compensate for eagerly anticipated flowers. In winter, night-time minimum temperatures of 10°C (50°F) are sufficient. Place the plants on a high shelf, close to the glass to get as much natural light as possible.

Tall-growing *D. nobile* hybrids may need support during their growth period or they can

BELOW
Dendrobium *Siam Jewel is an extremely popular warm-growing hard-caned Dendrobium. Various colours from white and pale pink, through to mauve and dark purple have been derived from species native to Australia. See page 136 for a full entry.*

ABOVE
The yellow-gold flowers and dark red-mauve lip of **Dendrobium** *Thongchai Gold make a stunning contrast. Hybrids such as this have been made possible due to the advancement of distinct breeding lines using Australian and New Guinea species. See page 135 for full entry.*

become top-heavy and be damaged by falling over. Grow the plants in as small a pot as possible (15cm/6in); they are sometimes overpotted to stop them becoming top-heavy but this can lead to overwatering, which may result in root loss and shrivelled pseudobulbs which cannot take up water. If a plant has become top-heavy, place the pot in a larger, heavier container.

Take care when repotting these orchids. It is a common fault to bury the base of the plant too deeply within the compost, so that the new growth starting from the base is

submerged and rots before it has a chance to develop. Always make sure the base of the plant is sitting on top of the compost. After repotting, tie the plant to a cane for support until the new roots anchor it firmly. Repot straight after flowering; these dendrobiums are not usually suitable for dividing and are better kept intact and dropped on (see page 210) where necessary into a slightly larger pot each time. The old, leafless canes can be used for propagating (see page 217) and the new plantlets grown on to flowering size within a few years. These orchids are semi-deciduous in cultivation and, when resting, tend to lose the leaves from one mature cane all at once in dramatic (though quite natural) fashion.

Other varieties

There is a smaller but no less charming group of dendrobiums known as the hirsute varieties because of their black-haired pseudobulbs. The best of this type is *Dendrobium infundibulum*, whose canes, or pseudobulbs are tall and slender, and the leaves dark green; flower nodes come from the upper half of the canes in spring. The plant is a native of India, Burma and Thailand, and will grow happily alongside the *D. nobile* types, requiring the same treatment summer and winter. Its large, showy flowers, which can be 8cm (3in) across the petals, are pristine white, soft and papery, with a deep yellow centre to the flared lip. These dendrobiums are less demanding of good light, so are well suited to indoor culture.

In addition there are many more varied types of dendrobium from India, whose flowers are as different from each other as are the plants. They are easily recognized by their typically tall canes, which in some species can exceed a metre (3 feet), and all require similar conditions, with as much variation in temperature between the summer growing season and the winter rest period as possible. While Indian dendrobiums were once plentiful and represented in most collections, today they are rare as importing restrictions have led to their decline in cultivation. Since many do not grow easily from seed, they cannot compete with the more easily raised *D. nobile* hybrids.

From Northern Australia and New Guinea come many ornate and distinct kinds, several uncommon in cultivation in other parts of the world. But there is one group, collectively known as *Phalaenopsis*-type dendrobiums because of the likeness of their flowers to those of the genus *Phalaenopsis*, popular for the amateur grower. Starting with the highly variable species, *D. bigibbum*, and others related to it, many colourful hybrids have been bred, all of which will grow in an intermediate greenhouse. *Phalaenopsis*-type dendrobiums produce elongated, hard-caned pseudobulbs (known as canes), with pairs of dark green, stiffened leaves along their length. They bloom from the top half of the leading cane, producing long stems that support a dozen or more showy flowers. These are usually rounded in shape, all parts of equal size, in colours ranging from white, through shades of light yellow, to rich mauve and purple combinations. The flowers are mostly self-coloured, or may be more deeply tinged towards the petal tips.

In cultivation the phalaenopsis-type plants like high light levels, combined with warmth (minimum winter temperature 13°C/55°F) and humidity. In spring, when they flower and produce new growths, give plenty of water at the roots; keep in a small pot (10cm/4in unless otherwise stated) and feed regularly over summer. Daytime temperatures can go as high as 30°C (85°F), provided the humidity is well balanced. Give just enough shading to prevent the leaves getting scorched. These orchids grow quickly, developing their canes within six months. Some become extremely tall, and with canes up to 90cm (3ft), they need plenty of headroom. On nearing completion, gradually reduce watering and increase the amount of light given, allowing the plants a total rest for winter. Dendrobiums should stay evergreen, shedding a few leaves but retaining most for another year or two.

Pleiones

This small genus of extremely popular, modest-growing deciduous orchids comes from China, the Himalayan regions of India as well as from Taiwan and Japan. The plants are mainly terrestrial, growing on moss-covered rocky outcrops and around the base of trees. They develop small, squat or cone-shaped pseudobulbs with a single leaf, shed in winter. The short-lived pseudobulbs become exhausted after one season and die naturally. Each new pseudobulb will produce several more every year, greatly increasing their number in a short time. These are usually grown together in a shallow pan and give a glorious show of flowers in early spring, though there are a few autumn-blooming species whose growing season is reversed from the norm. The flower spikes come from inside the new growth while it is very young, the thin stems supporting a single flower, rarely two, which are large for the size of plant, at 5–8cm (2–3in) across. The usual colourings are pink and white, sometimes yellow, but hybridizing within the genus has improved the colour range, the enriched pinks and mauves now vying for attention alongside pure white and apricot shades. While the sepals and petals are long and narrow, the lip is large and flared, fringed at its edge and attractively marked with darker colours.

Cultivation

Because of the ease with which these little plants grow, they are widely available from garden centres selling house-plants, sold as dormant bulbs ready for potting up. Grow pleiones in a soilless compost comprising equal parts of peat substitute and coarse sand or grit, with a little horticultural charcoal added. Repot annually as soon as the new growth is seen and before flowering, cutting off the oldest, dead pseudobulbs and the dead roots, leaving just enough to hold the new pseudobulbs and growth firmly in the pan. New roots will soon be seen just starting at the base of the new growth. Do not bury the pseudobulbs completely in the compost but allow them to settle on the surface. Though pan sizes are given for an individual plant, you can place as many as you like in a shallow pan, as pleiones prefer being crowded together.

After repotting, water carefully through a rose, but stop water getting into the funnel made by the new leaves. Keep the plants evenly watered all through summer, feeding lightly at every third watering, and gently mist the foliage on sunny days. As autumn becomes winter the leaves will turn yellow and drop: collect fallen leaves together with any surplus bulbils which have formed on the top of the mature pseudobulbs. Place the bulbils in a paper bag for the winter to pot up in spring. During winter, while the dormant bulbs are resting, leave completely dry and take them out of the pan or place it on a high, light shelf where they can stay until spring re-activates their growth. Overwinter these plants anywhere light and frost-free. They do not need the same minimum winter night temperatures as other cool-growing orchids: 5–7°C (40–45°F) suits them well.

During their summer growing season,

ABOVE
Pleione Versailles *is one of many attractive spring-flowering hybrids in this genus. The narrow, oval petals and sepals have a soft, glistening texture and the lip is large, frilled and delicately coloured at the centre, with streaks or spotting of a different colour.*

pleiones are intolerant of high temperatures and need to be kept cool at night, with daytime temperatures not exceeding 24°C (75°F). Where conditions are favourable, grow pleiones outdoors in a suitable bed or in containers sunk in the ground, bringing them back indoors for the winter – or grow them indoors on a cool windowsill or in an unheated cold frame; they look best grouped together, when their character shines through. Try to maintain the size of the pseudobulbs each year: if these become reduced and the plants stop flowering, they may have been grown too warm, or been given insufficient water while developing.

BELOW
With its widespread petals and sepals and generously coloured lip, gaily patterned with yellow striations and red dots, Pleione speciosa is typical of the genus. See page 110 for full entry.

Cattleya Alliance

Underlining the many natural and man-made genera horticulturally referred to as cattleyas is a complex web of interwoven hybrids comprising the largest group of related plants in the orchid family. As well as the naturally occurring *Cattleya* and *Sophronitis*, there are the man-made genera, of which *Sophrocattleya*, *Rhynchosophrocattleya,* and the large-flowered, delicate green *Rhyncholaelia* are the most notable. Other combinations have created a colossal variation but we restrict this section to those cattleyas popular for their ease of culture and availability.

Cattleyas and sophronitis are the two natural genera which appear most often in cultivation. Evergreen cattleyas produce pseudobulbs, from short (10cm/4in) to tall (90cm/3ft), along a visible strong rhizome. They are mainly club-shaped, sheathed and support either one leaf (unifoliate) or two (bifoliate). Both types produce rigid, oval to long leaves which are thick and leathery, while the flower spikes come from the apex of the pseudobulb at the base of the leaves. The short stems carry one to six large blooms up to 12cm (5in) across, which are among the most fabulous of all cultivated orchids. They are highly fragrant, and their subtle colourings include crisp white, buttercup yellow and the gorgeous hues of pink-purple, rich mauve and lavender, all with the colourful lip combinations at which these orchids excel.

The sophronitis are a similar genus, producing elongated, often slender pseudobulbs up to 30cm (12in) tall and a single oval, leathery leaf. Flower spikes, up to 30cm (12in) long, extend from the top of the pseudobulb and support up to eight attractive flowers in a similar colour range to that of the cattleyas. Most species within these two genera are autumn- or spring-flowering, their blooms lasting three weeks in perfection; the large-flowered types require some support (see below) to be seen at their best.

Cultivation

Balancing the temperature with humidity and moisture at the roots is the key to growing these exuberant orchids successfully. Use an open, swiftly draining compost made up of coarse bark, with an inert man-made material added to absorb water. Water cattleyas well while they are growing and feed every second or third watering.

When the buds first emerge from the top of the pseudobulb, they are enclosed by a green sheath; as they grow, they burst out from the sheath, splitting it along its length. In the weeks between the development of the sheath and the emergence of the buds, the sheath may become brown and wither, as it has a short lifespan; this will not affect the developing buds. Occasionally, the sheath fails to split, trapping the buds inside; you could, as a precaution, slit it open at the top. When the buds are left to open naturally, the flowers assume a nodding position and where there are two or more on the stem, they will crowd each other out. To prevent this, each bloom can be held in position by a slim bamboo cane, cut to a length where it will reach to just above the stem behind each flower when pushed into the compost; make a split in the top of each one, about 2cm (1in) long. Push a cane into the

ABOVE
*Sophrocattleya Persepolis is a bigeneric hybrid, the flower of which has full **Cattleya** shape and attractive, delicate colouring on the sepals and petals. See page 132 for a full entry.*

pot, then ease the flower stem into the slit; this will hold the flower firmly, without damaging it. You can now position the flower by twisting the cane in either direction. Do this with all flowers until the best position is reached, being careful not to snap the succulent stems. Alternatively, use horticultural string to tie each bloom to its support.

The roots of *Cattleya* are white, thick and rigid, and start to develop long after the new growth has started. The plants have two main growing seasons, spring and autumn, when the new roots will be active. When new roots start to grow, they produce an explosion of green tips at the base of the latest pseudobulb and, until they enter the compost, are vulnerable to damage and injury from slugs or snails. If the last pseudobulb has been made outside the pot's rim, the roots will progress down the outside of it, becoming aerial. Repot cattleyas after this new growth has started but before new roots are produced.

Hybrid cattleyas become large and bulky and are easiest to cope with in a greenhouse, where they have plenty of space and high humidity. They enjoy light overhead spraying in summer, but avoid getting water droplets on the flowers, which causes spotting of the paper-thin petals and sepals. Cattleyas like plenty of light, but not direct sunlight: shade them well in summer and give full light in winter. If you grow cattleyas indoors, select the compact kinds and give as much filtered light as possible all year round. In tropical countries they do well in the protection of a shade house, which allows a flow of fresh air at all times in a warm

temperature. Cattleyas need a minimum of 13°C (55°F) on winter nights; when exposed to prolonged lower temperatures their growth suffers, and ailments such as black spot can occur through being cold and damp. The maximum temperature is 30°C (85°F). Because much of the plant is covered with sheaths, cattleyas are prone to harbour scale insects, so when the sheaths have withered and dried, peel them off carefully, checking for these insects (see page 220). Cattleyas can rest for several weeks at a time, so when there is no sign of active growth, water just enough to prevent the pseudobulbs shrivelling. When large enough, cattleyas can be divided (see page 215), leaving at least four good pseudobulbs on each piece.

BELOW
Sophrocattleya Madge Fordyce 'Red Orb' takes its name from the two seperate genera that produced it. *Sophronitis* provides the brilliant colour and small pseudobulbs, with *Cattleya* contributing to the hybrid vigour.

Paphiopedilums and Phragmipediums

Commonly known as 'slipper orchids', to many people these are amongst the most fascinating groups of orchids to study. They are certainly the most diverse, having separated from the rest of the orchid family and developed their own distinct plant and flower structure. All carry their easily recognizable trademark, the pouch or slipper, which is a further modification of the third petal, or lip as it appears in other orchids. Their foliage and habit of growth are also unique. Originally we knew these orchids as *Cypripedium*, but today they are divided into three separate groups: *Paphiopedilum*, *Phragmipedium* and *Cypripedium*. While the first two are warm-growing, the terrestrial cypripediums require much cooler conditions; these orchids are not included here as they are extremely rare in cultivation, being occasionally found in specialist collections, which is where they belong.

Today all slipper orchids growing in the wild are considered endangered species and appear on the priority list of the authority for the Convention on International Trade in Endangered Species (CITES). In effect CITES ensures that no listed species can be imported or exported to anywhere in the world without a special licence proving that the plant has been nursery-raised and is not a wild-collected specimen. Despite this, their continuation in the wild is not entirely assured as their natural habitats continue to come under pressure from man's activities, including poaching.

Paphiopedilums

Paphiopedilums were one of the first tropical orchids to be widely cultivated and today they are still the most popular of the slipper orchids. These evergreen orchids, mainly terrestrial in the wild, produce growths consisting of two or more long and narrow, or oval, leaves, each new growth arising from the base of the previous one. Many species compensate for the lack of pseudobulbs by producing thicker, fleshy leaves whose foliage is mid- to dark green or mottled with lighter green; some leaves exhibit delicately peppered purple undersides. When the season's growth is completed, the flower bud emerges from the centre. Compared to other orchids, the rooting system of *Paphiopedilum* is sparse, the roots being brown and hairy. The plants vary in size from 8cm (3in) tall, or 15–30cm (6–12in) when in flower, to taller-growing types which may be 30cm (12in) tall in growth, with a flower spike that can reach up to 60cm (24in) in height.

Their flowers can last up to ten weeks, or longer where the sequential blooming of anything up to a dozen flowers in succession extends the flowering. Paphiopedilums also have the prettiest leaves of any orchid, and many are rewarding to grow for this attribute alone; those with mottled leaves make very attractive house-plants.

ABOVE
Phragmipedium Sedenii has inherited the light pastel colouring typical of older hybrids and in direct contrast to the bright colours of modern phragmipediums. See page 150 for full entry.

LEFT
This close-up of the pouch of the slipper orchid, **Paphiopedilum** *Jersey Freckles shows its extraordinary shape and elaborate patterning. See page 143 for full entry.*

Types of Paphiopedilum

Among the most popular types are the Complex hybrids, producing long, narrow, plain green leaves and a single large, rounded bloom. The flower can be self-coloured in peppery white, shining yellow or through a multitude of rich autumnal shades between brown and red. Or they may be heavily spotted and striped, with two or more different colours combined or overlaid to create a carnival of hues in high gloss. These wonderfully warm-toned flowers can last for months on end.

Then there is the Maudiae type of *Paphiopedilum*, single-flowered hybrids called after one of the first, and most delightful, hybrids made within this group. Their oval leaves are attractively mottled in green and grey-green, sometimes darkly peppered on the undersides, and their elegant flowers, carried proudly on tall, slender stems in summer, are green or red. The green-flowered kind are distinguished by their clear apple-green colouring, with the dorsal sepal humbug-striped. The red-flowered kind, with flamed dorsal sepals, can border on black, some of them an amazingly brooding, dark purple; these have a great following as growers strive to produce the elusive all-black flower.

A number of sequential-flowering species have been hybridized to produce pretty, compact blooms. The plants have elongated, light green leaves, and the flowers appear on long stems which gradually extend as buds open in succession over a period of several months. The main colourings in this group are clear shades of cornfield yellow and tan leading towards light orange, with a sprinkling of brown or purple. Bright and cheerful, these little plants have a captivating charm.

The last group, known as the Rothschildianum group, have the most dramatically stunning flowers of all. These hybrids, raised from species which inhabit Borneo and the Philippines, have no equal: their flowers are distinguished by the long, ribbon-like petals which can extend almost vertically or swivel horizontally for up to 15cm (6in). The plants are large and robust, their long leaves mid- to dark green. In flower, their tall spikes may attain a height of a metre (3 feet) or more, the blooms, four to six on a stem, opening all together; they will remain for weeks during the spring and summer months, their colouring striking, almost unreal combinations of near-black and purple lines on a white base. While these dramatic plants are greatly sought after, unfortunately they are extremely slow to breed and to grow.

Cultivation

In cultivation different paphiopedilums will all grow under one roof, which is surprising as the species come from many different climates. With the occasional exception, their needs are the same and a well-shaded greenhouse with a minimum winter night-time temperature of 18°C (64°F) will suit them. Without pseudobulbs, they are unable to cope with long periods of drought, so keep them evenly moist all year round, slightly drier in winter. The plants grow steadily, slowing down in winter, but do not have a true rest period. Pot into an open, well-drained compost, using as small a pot as possible. Complex types benefit from annual repotting with little disturbance to the root system, often returning plants to the same size pot. Spray lightly in summer but do not allow water to run down into the centre of the growth, where it may cause rot.

Phragmipediums

Of the three genera discussed that make up the slipper orchids, *Phragmipedium* is the smallest group. But although it contains the least species, these are highly collectible and excite great interest. Phragmipediums are usually terrestrial, although a few can grow overhanging water. In these situations the plants contend with daily downpours or thunderstorms which continually drench them. Because they grow in a well-draining situation, with water moving through the roots very fast, the constant wetting is not a problem – a point to remember when watering these orchids at home.

Bearing some resemblance to the paphiopedilums, these plants are usually more tufted and vigorous in growth, producing strap-like leaves from 10cm (4in) to 90cm (3ft) long. Their tall flower spikes are sequential blooming so that within a few days of the first flower suddenly dropping off, a second and third will replace it, to continue in this way for months. It is normal for one flower spike to keep producing blooms for 18 months to two years. While a few species bear rounded flowers, similar to paphiopedilums, with the typical pouch, the flowers are mostly large and spiky, with long, narrow, pointed petals which droop impressively to suggest their common name, mandarin orchids. These eye-catching blooms, up to 15cm (6in) across, are found in a blend of pastel greens and leafy browns, while the smaller, rounded blooms can be a pretty shell-pink; the pink varieties were eagerly sought by the early hybridizers.

Cultivation

Phragmipediums thrive in various potting mediums but the most successful is the inert man-made fibre, Rockwool, which allows the plants to be kept wetter through the year with no danger of rotting, as with organic compost. Artificial feed must be applied regularly to encourage a steady rate of growth for these lush plants, which can even be stood in a tray of water to ensure their roots are continually wet – which would spell instant death to any other orchid! Apart from their liking for wet conditions at the roots, phragmipediums can be grown in the same way as paphiopedilums (see page 47), in a warm, well-shaded greenhouse with year-round care and the same minimum temperature.

BELOW
Phragmipedium besseae
was only discovered in 1980, when its vibrant red colouring caused a sensation. See page 152 for full entry.

Epidendrums

Until it became apparent that there were in fact many separate genera, the first orchids to be recognized and classified all went under the name *Epidendrum*, which means simply 'upon a tree' and referred to the orchids' epiphytic habit of attaching themselves to trees as an anchor upon which to grow. Among the epidendrums grown today are the first known tropical orchids, discovered over 200 years ago.

Those orchids remaining in the genus *Epidendrum* are extremely interesting and colourful plants, distributed throughout tropical America; they are mainly tall-growing, with slender, reed-like canes and foliage. The flowers come from the top of the growth and there may be from a few to hundreds, one inflorescence producing successive blooms over many months. The blooms are quite small, seldom more than 2cm (1in) across, but often make up for their lack of size in quantity. Some, like the red-flowered *E. radicans*, become perpetually blooming on a specimen plant which can reach 1.5m (5ft). They are most at home in tropical gardens, where they grow large, their colours ranging from yellow, orange and red to green, brown, white or pink.

Plant the tall-growing species in a bed at one end of an intermediate greenhouse, where there is enough headroom, in a mixture of bark chippings or peat and charcoal. As the plants grow they make copious aerial roots and self-propagate readily from the apex

of old stems. Repotting or re-bedding is needed only if the plant outgrows its site – otherwise propagations can just be removed and potted up. A smaller group of epidendrums produce the familiar pseudobulbs, tall and slender, with a pair of rigid, long and oval leaves. The flowers, which come from the apex of the pseudobulbs, are mostly green with narrow petals and sepals dominated by a white, three-lobed lip, sometimes frilled along its edge, as in *E. ciliare* (see page 160 for full entry). Watering and regular spraying, applying feed at every third watering, is all these fascinating orchids need to keep them in good health.

ABOVE
Epidendrum pseudepidenrum belongs to the reed-type epidendrums. It produces several flowers with bright orange waxy lips that are almost plastic in appearance. For full entry see page 159.

LEFT
*The shape of the flowers on this brightly coloured **Epidendrum radicans** give rise to its common name of crucifix orchid. Its popularity has soared in recent years with the introduction of 'compact' varieties.*

RIGHT
*The white-flowered species **Epidendrum parkinsonium** produces heavy, spear-shaped leaves that hang down from diminutive pseudobulbs.*

Phalaenopsis

Phalaenopsis have undergone a phenomenal rise in popularity in recent decades. Among the first of the tropical orchids to gain favour in Victorian collections, the species were cultivated for their attractive flowers on long, branching stems, but only a few were considered desirable and hybridizing with these was slow and unrewarding. For many years, therefore, little or no advancement was made, though the species were commonly sought after.

Horticulturally, the genus *Phalaenopsis* can be loosely divided into two types. There are those with long, often branching spikes and large, softly textured, well-rounded blooms in pastel shades of pink and white. The other group carry their flowers on a shortened spike, producing less rounded, waxy flowers with brighter colourings. Intensive breeding between the two groups has caused them to merge into a great family of superb hybrids, with dazzling colours and variations once thought impossible. This modern hybridizing has revolutionized the genus, carrying it to the pinnacle of success.

The best *Phalaenopsis* hybrids have been extended to include combinations of white petals and sepals with highly decorative lips in red and orange, while the pinks have been developed to encompass the richest shades of purple. Though generally self-coloured, the pastel pinks and whites may be overlaid with candy stripes, or spotted or dusted with darker colours. Yellow colouring has also come to the fore and you can now find pure or spotted yellows, sometimes bordering on lime or gold. The smallest of the yellow hybrids carry numerous flowers, 2cm (1in) across, on spikes under 30cm (12in) tall. For ease of growing and regular flowering, these orchids have no equal, which is why more phalaenopsis are being raised throughout the world today than any other orchid. The species are still grown in specialist collections and individual plants can be found in dedicated orchid nurseries, while the hybrids are available in their thousands from outlets that include florists and garden centres.

Cultivation

Phalaenopsis grow steadily throughout the year, slowing down during winter in response to shorter daylight hours and lower temperatures and speeding up in spring and summer. Their seasons are less marked than in other orchids, making them easier to handle as a house-plant; they also adapt more readily to drier conditions. Indoors they are happy in a position of semi-shade, well away from direct sunlight but in a warm area where there is little fluctuation between day and night, summer and winter temperatures. The plants grow equally well in a warm greenhouse, with a minimum winter night temperature of 18°C (64°F), rising in the day by at least 4–5°C (10°F), while in summer temperatures as high as 30°C (85°F) will not harm them.

Lightly spray or mist *Phalaenopsis* leaves in summer, but keep water out of the centre, where it will cause rotting if left. Discontinue spraying in winter, when the water can remain for too long on the leaf surface; the leaves of indoor plants may be sponged over. Few pests attack phalaenopsis, although aphids may

congregate on the developing flower spikes and buds, and false red spider mite can affect the leaves (see page 220). The most vulnerable part of these plants is the centre crown from which the new leaves emerge. Rots caused by cold or wet conditions can start here, usually in winter when the plants are more at risk. In this case the centre leaf will pull away and be brown and wet at the base. Once the centre has rotted, the plant often attempts to grow again from near the base, producing a healthy new plant by the side of the original, the leaves on the older plant eventually turning yellow and dropping off. If no new growth appears within six weeks, the plant is likely to die.

Repot phalaenopsis in spring or autumn, while they are not in flower; leave any aerial roots outside the container, trimming them back if damaged. As phalaenopsis do not make extensive roots within the pot, you can often return them to the same size container once all dead roots have been removed. Some species of

Phalaenopsis naturally grow downward, their long leaves becoming pendant and hanging free; this assists drainage and prevents the centre of the plant from filling with water.

Phalaenopsis flowers last for many weeks in perfection, and when the last bloom has faded and dropped from the stem, this can be cut back to a lower node, so that within a few weeks a secondary flowering stem will grow from below the cut to prolong the flowering. A single mature plant can remain in bloom indefinitely, as new flower spikes replace the older ones before they have finished (see page 221). With just a small selection of plants, you can achieve flowers all year round.

ABOVE
With its neatly arching flower spikes and up to a dozen blooms with overlapping petals, **Phalaenopsis** *Happy Girl is the classic hybrid and is very popular for floral displays.*

Vanda Alliance

Vandas produce the most gorgeous, brightly coloured blooms and would undoubtedly be grown by everyone were the plants as easy to accommodate as they are beautiful. Their gaudy colours reflect the tropical climate and year-round sunshine with which their cultivation is synonymous. They readily interbreed with closely related genera, including *Euanthe*, *Ascocentrum* and others, to produce the multitude of coveted hybrids grown today. All are monopodial orchids, producing pairs of long, semi-rigid leaves from an upright, ever-growing rhizome. The plants can grow tall, up to a metre (3 feet), with long, stiffened aerial roots descending well below it. Though evergreen, they lose their foliage occasionally, one or two leaves at a time. The flower spikes appear from the base of a lower leaf and grow speedily to produce up to twelve, more usually about six, large, flamboyant flowers, varying in size from 5–15cm (2–6in). Their glamorous rounded petals overlap the sepals, while the lip is tiny by comparison. They bloom at various times, with peak flowering in spring and early summer.

Unusually among orchids, vandas' most prominent colour is blue, which may be pale sky to deep violet, the colouring mottled or tessellated over a lighter tone. Other colours include mauves and purples, and breeding with related genera has produced vibrant reds, fiery oranges and yellows bordering on green, with all hues in between. But it is the coveted blue for which these orchids are best known.

Cultivation

Outside of the tropics vandas do not make good house-plants, and will only be found in specialist nurseries where a limited selection may be offered. Their cultivation indoors often leads to disappointment where the drier atmosphere and inaccessibility to year-long light greatly inhibits their growth, and where they are liable to rapid dehydration. But in a warm greenhouse with a sunny aspect vandas can be tried by enthusiastic growers willing to rise to the challenge of growing these demanding but very rewarding orchids. Some vandas are more adaptable than others and the fabled *Vandanthe* Rothschildiana, with its huge, blue flowers, and its hybrids are the outstanding exception. They can be grown and flowered with comparable ease, even in the less sunny climates of Britain and parts of Europe. This *Vandanthe* is a primary hybrid first raised in 1931, since when the cross has been repeated many times. On one side is *Vanda coerulea*, a soft sky-blue-flowered plant growing high in the Himalayas, where cold nights are normal through part of the year, while the other parent is *Euanthe sanderiana*, a warm-growing species native to the Philippines. The resulting cross has created a plant with an unusually wide temperature tolerance, enabling it to be grown the world over.

In summer vandas enjoy a sunny aspect and high humidity in a greenhouse where the temperature does not drop below 16–18°C (60–64°F) at night. During the day this can rise safely to 30°C (85°F), with a significant increase in humidity to match the tropical environment as nearly as possible. These temperatures should be adhered to closely, even in winter. Grown well, the plants will

ABOVE
Cut flowers, such as this **Vandanthe** *Memoria Lyle Swanson 'Justin Grannel', are flown around the world in water tubes, to ensure the orchids stay fresh. See page 193 for full entry.*

LEFT
A close-up of **Schlechterara** *Blue Boy 'Indigo' shows the small lip that is typical of the alliance and used as a platform by alighting insects. See page 190 for full entry.*

flower several times in a year, but this reward may prove elusive. Vandas may be grown conventionally in pots or half pots (12cm/5in) but, better still, in open, slatted wooden baskets. Fill the basket with chunky pieces of bark and horticultural charcoal, a mix which is firm enough to support the plant and hold it in the container. Ideally, hang the baskets near to the glass in the greenhouse roof, where it is also warmer in winter. This mode of growing allows the long aerial roots to extend downward, where they can grow to over 90cm (3ft) long. Watering is best done by regular, twice-daily spraying, misting the entire plant and its roots. As the temperature falls towards evening, the humidity will rise naturally,

benefiting the plants which need not be sprayed again until the next morning, to allow time for any water lodging in the funnel-shaped tip of the plant to dry out; this part is vulnerable to rot. In this case new growth will be made from lower down the plant but it will be several years before it blooms. In addition to spraying, foliar feed regularly throughout the year, so the plants can absorb the extra nutrients through their thick leaves and aerial roots.

As a plant extends upwards along the vertical rhizome, the bottom part will become a bare stem, the lower leaves being shed

ABOVE
*This unusual trigeneric hybrid, **Christieara** Renée Gerber 'Fuchs Confetti', produces distinctive blooms on dense, upright flower spikes. See page 197 for full entry.*

naturally. In time there can be more stem than plant in leaf, at which stage the stem can be cut, separating the leafed part of the plant, together with a good supply of aerial roots, to pot up on its own. If kept, the base of the plant may produce new growth too. This is about the only time a *Vanda* needs repotting, otherwise it can remain in its basket and have the compost replaced without being removed from it. If the plant has outgrown its basket, place it and the plant directly into a larger one, filling in the space around with the same chunky potting materials.

Vandas have a short resting period during the winter. It is noticeable when the green tips of the roots cease to grow and become covered by the papery white velamen which affords protection to the exposed root and, being porous, absorbs moisture and nutrients. Pests seldom attack vandas when grown in these humid conditions, but their roots are vulnerable to slug damage.

From among a large number of closely related orchids which interbreed with vandas, ascocentrums are the most significant. Requiring similar growing conditions to vandas, they are similar in appearance but more compact and shorter growing. Their flowers are equally bright and, when crossed with vandas to produce ascocendas, the results are stunning, with many more flowers on a spike in greatly enhanced colourings. These jewels of the orient are hard to resist but remain one of the great challenges to orchid growers today.

ABOVE
The twisted stems of **Schlechterara** *Fuchs Sunkist 'Mike' (above), another intergeneric hybrid, show how the flowers turn before opening to a position where their lips are displayed horizontally. See page 190 for full entry.*

Cool-growing orchids

The vast majority of orchids grown today come from among the cool-growing types as their cultivation is often easier as well as their heat requirements less. Many growers restrict their collection entirely to cool-growing hybrids without in any way limiting the abundance of variety, such is the huge choice available without having to provide the extra warmth required by intermediate and warm-growing orchids. Cool-growing orchids include those, like cymbidiums and odontoglossums, that live at high altitudes in the wild. Most grow easily indoors provided they are not exposed to excesses of temperature such as may occur in a conservatory, which can over-heat in summer, or an area left unheated in winter. Choose a well-lit part of a living room which is not directly in the sun; it should be warm by day and cool at night.

Cymbidium Maureen Grapes 'Marilyn'

This fresh, spring-green clone has retained all the original hues from the species, *Cymbidium ensiflorum*, which produced the highly acclaimed Peter Pan, a parent of Maureen Grapes. The sweet fragrance has continued through this special breeding line, developed in New Zealand to fill a gap in the flowering season of cymbidiums. The blooms are 5cm (2in) wide, the dense red peppering on the lip also indicative of the species. This cymbidium is sequential flowering, with spikes developing at different stages to give a succession of blooms over a long period. Since its first appearance in 1984, this hybrid has been a favourite, unbeatable for its summer flowering.

FLOWER
5cm (2in) wide

FLOWER SPIKE
90cm (36in) long

PLANT
45cm (18 in) high

POT SIZE
15cm (6in)

Cymbidium Valley Blush 'Magnificent'

This is a standard-type *Cymbidium* clone capable of producing up to a dozen large, dramatic flowers per spike, each with clear, spring-green colouring and a delicately spotted lip. Several spikes appear on a large plant. These green-flowered hybrids require good light to initiate the flower spikes in late summer but, once the buds begin to show, they need to be given more shade. Over-exposure to light at this stage can cause the buds to abort, turning yellow and dropping off just when you expect them to open. Once in bloom, keep the plant in shade to prolong the flowering and maintain the colour.

FLOWER
10cm (4in) wide

FLOWER SPIKE
120cm (48in) long

PLANT
100cm (40in) high

POT SIZE
20cm (8in)

Cymbidium Tangerine Mary

Raised in New Zealand, this latest winter-flowering cymbidium is a breakthrough into the vibrant colours once seen only in the later, mid-season hybrids. Produced for the home grower, the plant is compact, with its leaves held upright, and is less demanding of space than most cymbidiums. The flower spikes carry numerous flowers, held naturally upright and reaching no taller than the foliage. A mature plant blooms freely through winter, producing flower spikes which open in succession.

FLOWER
5cm (2in) wide

FLOWER SPIKE
90cm (36in) long

PLANT
60cm (24in) high

POT SIZE
15cm (6in)

Cymbidium Cotil Point AM/RHS

Cotil Point is an eye-catching hybrid, bred in Jersey in the late 1990s, one of the latest in a long line of superb red-flowered hybrids giving a wonderful depth of colour with quality and substance of flower. It is winning awards on both sides of the Atlantic and has already gained three awards of merit from the Royal Horticultural Society in London. The striping on the petals and sepals, often seen in the red-flowered hybrids, expresses the influence of the Indian species *C. tracyanum*, a brown and tan striped flower with a yellow lip. Although used far back in the pedigree of this plant, its contribution is clear. The large flowers open during the winter and can be left on the plant for their duration, or cut singly.

FLOWER
15cm (6in) wide

FLOWER SPIKE
120cm (48in) long

PLANT
100cm (40in) high

POT SIZE
20cm (8in)

Cymbidium Bruttera

FLOWER
5cm (2in) wide

FLOWER SPIKE
90cm (36in) long

PLANT
30cm (12in) high

POT SIZE
15cm (6in)

This attractive compact hybrid is among the first to bloom after the
summer growing season. Free-flowering throughout autumn, it carries a
refreshing fragrance to complement its clear colouring; a medium-sized
plant can yield up to six flower spikes. To ensure a good crop of flowers,
place Bruttera outdoors for the summer growing season, which will
produce a harder growth. Once the flower spikes, resembling fat
pencils, are seen at the base of the plant, bring it indoors into a light
position, where it will flower for weeks.

Cymbidium Cotil Point 'Ridgeway'

Some degree of variation is present with all orchid hybrids but it is even more noticeable in cymbidiums. Any number of clones from a particular hybrid will show differences in colour, shape and lip markings. There are so many conflicting genes in the make-up of modern hybrids that any one can appear dominant in a flower. Cotil Point 'Ridgeway' shows considerable variation from the hybrid illustrated on page 62. The similarities are the striped petals and sepals, and the shape of the lip, while the main difference lies in the colouring, which is noticeably lighter in 'Ridgeway'.

FLOWER
15cm (6in) wide

FLOWER SPIKE
120cm (48in) long

PLANT
100cm (40in) high

POT SIZE
20cm (8in)

Cymbidium Bethlehem

This white, midwinter-flowering cymbidium can trace its long pedigree back to two white species, *C. eburneum*, a single-flowered plant from India and Burma, and *C. erythrostyllum*, a multi- but smaller-flowered species from Vietnam. The influence of the former was to give good shape, but few flowers, on the early white hybrids. That of the latter, and other breeding plants, helped to overcome this problem to give the long spikes of the modern white hybrids. This Californian-bred hybrid has the slightest blush of pink touching the sepals, while the petals carry a light adornment, highlighted in greater detail on the prettily marked lip. To ensure the plant blooms well the following year, place out of doors for the summer months to produce a strong growth which will ripen well before producing its flower spikes.

FLOWER
12cm (5in) wide

FLOWER SPIKE
120cm (48in) long

PLANT
100cm (40in) high

POT SIZE
20cm (8in)

Cymbidium Glowing Valley 'Sunrise'

Behind the majority of all standard hybrids is the most famous cymbidium of all time, Alexanderi 'Westonbirt' FCC/RHS. The influence of this white hybrid, raised in 1922, can still be seen today in the shape and substance of flowers like Glowing Valley, raised in 1985 from the finest Australian stock. This perfectly shaped flower has a hint of shell-pink with a delicately spotted lip, creating a subtle counterpoint to the bolder colourings found in the genus. The very pale coloured flowers can be spoilt by too much bright light and, while they are in bloom, should be kept away from direct sunlight, when they will last in perfection for up to ten weeks.

FLOWER
9cm (3¹/₂in) wide

FLOWER SPIKE
120cm (48in) long

PLANT
100cm (40in) high

POT SIZE
20cm (8in)

Cymbidium Valley Splash 'Awesome'

Many of the best *Cymbidium* hybrids are raised in Australia, which has become the breeding centre of the world for this particular variety of orchid. All those with 'Valley' in their names are from the Valley Orchids nursery in South Australia; Valley Splash appeared in 1991. The brushed petals and sepals on this lovely hybrid give an unusual bi-coloured large flower which is slightly cupped.

FLOWER
l0cm (4in) wide

FLOWER SPIKE
120cm (48in) long

PLANT
100cm (40in) high

POT SIZE
20cm (8in)

FLOWER
10cm (4in) wide

FLOWER SPIKE
120cm (48in) long

PLANT
90cm (36in) high

POT SIZE
30cm (12in)

Cymbidium Nevada

Cymbidiums such as this superb standard yellow hybrid have been cultivated and hybridized for over 100 years. This modern hybrid produces 1.2-m (4-ft) long upright flower spikes in spring, each with a dozen or more blooms. A mature plant can easily carry up to six flower spikes, 10cm (4in) wide, producing a fantastic display lasting for weeks. The flower spikes first appear in autumn, and as the summer's pseudobulbs mature, they grow steadily throughout the winter. As the stems lengthen, they need support to prevent them snapping under their own weight. Grow these plants, 90cm (36in) high without flower spikes, in a 30cm (12in) pot. They need plenty of headroom and are best suited to cultivation in a greenhouse or conservatory where there is good light all year. If space allows you to grow them indoors, they can spend the summer outside to benefit from the extra light needed to encourage the flowers.

Cymbidium Mini Sarah 'Sunburst'

With a pretty white- and yellow-spotted lip, this is one of a wide range of compact orchids produced to give a shorter plant with smaller flowers, more easily accommodated indoors. Mini Sarah is a direct descendant of the Formosan species, *C. floribundum*, a compact-growing, small-flowered orchid. It was overlooked for many years as a potential breeding plant but from the late 1950s has been used extensively to create the miniature types so useful for indoor growing. Several flower spikes can be produced in one season, not all opening at the same time, giving an extended season of bloom. Flowering can carry on through the winter months, well into the spring, during which time the plant needs to be watered and fed regularly to maintain the extra effort required. Repot as soon as possible after flowering. These smaller plants can be left undivided for several years without ever becoming too large to manage easily.

FLOWER
9cm (3¹/₂in) wide

FLOWER SPIKE
60cm (24in) long

PLANT
75cm (30in) high

POT SIZE
20cm (8in)

Rhynchostele bictoniensis

This Guatemalan species, introduced in 1835, has produced a line of attractive hybrids under its former name, *Odontoglossum*, particularly with related genera such as *Brassia* (see pages 114–115), but it remains a collectable species in its own right. By using the predominantly pale-lipped alba, or darker forms, hybrids in yellow and pink-red can be raised. Long-lasting flowers, carried on an upright spike, form in two rows along the stem. Lightly shade the plant during summer, when the plant blooms with its growing nearly complete. It forms large clumps within a few years. Water throughout the year, though only lightly in winter.

GROWERS' TIP
The tall, slender flower spikes will need supporting to keep them upright.

FLOWER
4cm (1¹/₂in) wide

FLOWER SPIKE
45cm (18in) long

PLANT
30cm (12in) high

POT SIZE
12cm (5in) high

Rhynchostele bictoniensis x *Brassia* **Stardust**

Not all the hybrids within the *Odontoglossum* alliance produce the typical, well-rounded flowers with wide petals and sepals and this new hybrid is one of the novelty crosses within this highly variable group. As yet unnamed, it carries the names of its parents for identification. *Brassia* Stardust is a long-petalled, green-flowered type of spider orchid, so-called for its narrow, elongated petals. While the species has provided the long flowering spike with numerous flowers, the Stardust hybrid has increased the size and intensified the colour of this charming cross. Though it needs light shade in summer, it will tolerate a slightly higher maximum temperature of 30°C (85°F). Breeding from *R. bictoniensis* has given rise to some other extremely colourful, summer-blooming odontoglossums. These hybrids usually have a rest period in winter, when they can be kept dry and in full light until new growth is seen.

Odontiopsis Boussole 'Blanche'

Here is a French-bred intergeneric hybrid of exceptional quality, the result of crossing *Miltoniopsis* with *Odontoglossum*. Most odontiopsis possess the large, flamboyant lip of the *Miltoniopsis* parent but, in this instance, the *Odontoglossum* proves to be dominant. The star-shaped flowers with pointed petals can be traced back to the species *O. crispum*, which has produced all the modern white hybrids. The flared lip and slight pink tinging on the inside of the flower come from its pink-flowered parent, *Miltonia vexillaria*; the coloration is deeper on the outside. This hybrid has a long pedigree, however, with several other clones contributing through successive generations to the overall excellence of Boussole 'Blanche'.

FLOWER
8cm (3in) wide

FLOWER SPIKE
30cm (12in) long

PLANT
30cm (12in) high

POT SIZE
10cm (4in)

Rhynchlioglossum Kalkastern

Kalkastern is a recent German-bred hybrid, achieved by using the dark red *Odontioda* Feuerkugel with the species *Rhynchostele rossii* to give a wonderfully coloured, compact flower with a broad lip. The blue-mauve colour of the lip is greatly sought after in this type of hybrid and here the rich yellow honey guide clearly shows at the centre of the blooms. The advantage of this breeding line is its departure from the more usual rounded, small-lipped flowers, to give a perfectly balanced but overall smaller flower well-suited to indoor growing. *Rhynchostele rossii* has been successfully crossed with variously coloured hybrids, extending the range of colours while retaining the qualities seen here.

FLOWER
5cm (2in) wide

FLOWER SPIKE
20cm (8in) long

PLANT
30cm (12in) high

POT SIZE
10cm (4in)

Odontioda Marie Noel 'Bourgogyne'

FLOWER
6cm (2¹/₂in) wide

FLOWER SPIKE
30cm (12in) long

PLANT
30cm (12in) high

POT SIZE
10cm (4in)

The most highly patterned orchids of all can be found among the *Odontoglossum* hybrids. This is one of a long line of superb crosses from the long-established, world-renowned orchid nursery of Vacherot & Lecoufle in France. Hybrids such as Marie Noel have won many awards for outstanding quality and 'Bourgogyne' is one of the finest clones, with its distinctive leopard spotting on the flowers. Their origins, which can be traced back through many generations to the lovely white species, *Odontoglossum crispum*, can still be seen in the crisp, highly ornate white flowers, although they may also be self-coloured in almost any shade, except blue or green. The species comes from the Andean mountains of South America where it grows on trees at high altitudes and enjoys cool nights and fresh mountain breezes. The well-rounded blooms, with sepals and petals of equal size, have a small, neat lip which usually carries similar adornment to the rest of the flower.

Odyncidium Hansueli Isler

The brilliant patterning and colourful
arrangement of red-brown overlaid on a
yellow base is seen even through the buds of
this delightful, German-bred hybrid. Several
modern hybrids are named to honour
members of the Swiss Isler family, whose head,
Jakob Isler, is a commercial grower. One of
Europe's leading hybridizers, he has produced a
number of fine modern crosses within the
Odontoglossum alliance. This plant, with its
ornate lip, is very free-flowering, producing
sturdy, upright spikes with six to ten blooms
on the stem. These are long-lasting but should
be kept out of direct sunlight and away from
excessive heat while in bloom, as temperature
extremes can cause the fine-looking blooms to
wilt prematurely.

FLOWER
6cm (2¹/2in) wide

FLOWER SPIKE
50cm (20in) long

PLANT
30cm (12in) high

POT SIZE
10cm (4in)

Odontocidium Isler's Goldregen

The introduction of *Oncidium* adds a further dimension to the *Odontoglossum* alliance. Oncidiums have a predominance of yellow-flowered species, and it is these species (including the much bred-from *O. tigrinum*) which, crossed with yellow odontoglossums, result in some wonderfully rich browns and yellows. Here, the heavy, reddish brown overlay almost completely obscures the yellow base colour. This large flower has a precise star shape to the petals and sepals, while the generous lip is flared, an *Oncidium* feature. Some of these hybrids can produce very tall flower spikes which, with their well-sized blooms, are extremely eye-catching. The robust plants produce big pseudobulbs which will bloom at almost any time of year.

FLOWER
8cm (3in) wide

FLOWER SPIKE
60cm (24in) long

PLANT
30cm (12in) high

POT SIZE
10cm (4in)

Odontocidium Purbeck Gold

This is an older type of British-bred hybrid, first produced in 1983. Still in great demand for its exquisite colouring and large, flared lip, it produces a robust plant with tall flower spikes, which blooms mainly in the autumn, its yellow and brown colouring perfectly matching the season. The rich yellow is a direct result of using the distinctive Mexican species, *Oncidium tigrinum* as a parent. This strongly textured plant carries the yellow flared lip characterizing all its progeny. The hybrids also inherit the large pseudobulbs, making them excellent, free-blooming growers, often producing two flower spikes from a single pseudobulb. Regular repotting helps the plant reach its full potential. Odontocidiums can also be red, red-brown and red-mauve in colouring depending on the breeding lines.

FLOWER
6cm (2½in) wide

FLOWER SPIKE
50cm (20in) long

PLANT
30cm (12in) high

POT SIZE
10cm (4in)

Wilsonara Uruapan 'Tyrone' AM/RHS

There is as much variation to be found among the wilsonaras as among any of the man-made intergeneric hybrids within the *Odontoglossum* alliance. *Wilsonara* is the result of crossing three natural genera, *Cochlioda*, *Odontoglossum* and *Oncidium*. The first of this trigeneric cross, named after Mr Gurney Wilson, an eminent orchidist and writer of his day, was flowered in 1916. Very few new wilsonaras were raised until the introduction of *Oncidium tigrinum* revitalized the genus, creating wonderfully rich combinations, as seen here. They are a fitting testimonial to a man who was awarded the Victoria Medal of Honour by the Royal Horticultural Society in London, for his services to orchidology. This attractive and beautifully symmetrical flower shows the greatest influence of the *Cochlioda* and *Odontoglossum* within the breeding. A strong and robust grower, it produces tall flower spikes with up to a dozen blooms on the stem. Its flowering season varies throughout the year.

FLOWER
9cm (3¹/2in) wide

FLOWER SPIKE
50cm (20in) long

PLANT
25cm (10in) high

POT SIZE
15cm (6in)

Wilsonara Widecombe Fair

This captivating pink and white hybrid is the result of using different species within the *Odontoglossum* alliance to give a smaller, more open style of flower. While the plant is typical of odontoglossums, the flower spike is taller, carrying numerous flowers on side branches. The species, *Oncidium incurvum* has imparted its characteristically long spike and flower shape to the hybrid in a superior form. On the other side of its parentage stands *Odontioda* Florence Stirling, much used in the 1940s and 1950s to endow its progeny with its rich purple colouring. The tall, summer-flowering spikes take months to grow and develop their blooms and need supporting from a young age. Widecombe Fair is a vigorous hybrid which grows just as well in a warmer environment of 13°C (55°F) minimum, if daytime temperatures are kept below 24°C (75°F). This has enabled it to succeed in hot parts of the USA, such as Florida, Texas and California, where cool shade can be provided.

FLOWER
5cm (2in) wide

FLOWER SPIKE
90cm (36in) long

PLANT
23cm (9in) high

POT SIZE
10cm (4in)

Wilsonara Kolibri

The *Oncidium* parent has had the greatest influence on this trigeneric hybrid by reducing the flower size but greatly increasing the number of flowers on the spike. These are carried on side branches, giving a pleasing 'Christmas tree' effect. The pink and red colouring of the petals and sepals comes from *Cochlioda*, while the overall shape, although reduced, is typical *Odontoglossum*. This unusual breeding line successfully incorporated the best varieties of the pretty pink and white, tall-stemmed species *Oncidium incurvum*, with the smaller, dainty-flowered *Oncidium ornithorhynchum* two generations back, showing how different flowers can be produced to create further variety within the *Odontoglossum* alliance.

FLOWER
4cm (1½in) wide

FLOWER SPIKE
100cm (40in) long

PLANT
18cm (7in) high

POT SIZE
15cm (6in)

Odonchlopsis Cambria 'Yellow'

This is the yellow variety of Cambria 'Plush' (see right). Cambria has four instances of the highly variable species *Odontoglossum harryanum* in its early ancestry and this has influenced the hybrid to the extent that during the mass cloning process tissue-coloured variants were accidentally produced. One of these, *Odonchlopsis* Cambria 'Yellow', appeared a few years ago in Holland and has since gone on to reproduce true to its colour; this freak occurrence has made the plant popular. In all other respects Cambria 'Yellow' is identical to Cambria 'Plush'.

FLOWER
8cm (3in) wide

FLOWER SPIKE
50cm (20in) long

PLANT
30cm (12in) high

POT SIZE
12cm (5in)

Odonchlopsis Cambria 'Plush' FCC/RHS

This is probably the most popular orchid of all time within the *Odontoglossum* alliance, due to its large, strikingly beautiful, flamboyant flowers, its willingness to bloom and its ease of growing. Cambria first appeared in 1931, originating from the famous British nursery of Charlesworth & Co. at Hayward's Heath in Surrey, England. With the advent of meristem culture, its popularity spread worldwide and today it can be found in every country where orchids are cultivated. It was awarded its first class certificate in 1967. The

FLOWER
8cm (3in) wide

FLOWER SPIKE
50cm (20in) long

PLANT
30cm (12in) high

POT SIZE
12cm (5in)

plant will bloom twice a year, often producing two flower spikes from one pseudobulb, with up to a dozen long-lasting blooms on each one. Ensure that the pseudobulbs remain in a plump state and are not allowed to get so dry that they become shrivelled.

Sanderara Rippon Tor 'Burnham'

The trigeneric hybrid, produced by crossing *Brassia*, *Cochlioda* and *Odontoglossum*, is named after the founder of the famous nursery of Sander & Sons of St Albans, England. The first of the genus was registered in 1937. The *Brassia* influence has lengthened and narrowed the sepals and petals to give a more open flower, which is otherwise typical *Odontoglossum* and reminiscent of the earlier hybrids most closely allied to the species. The attractive flowers are produced on a tall, arching stem with up to a dozen large blooms. Their ivory-white base colour is overlaid with splashes of red and pink on the sepals and petals, intensified at the centre of the creamy yellow lip. Its flowering time is various, but it blooms mostly during spring. The plant is tall and robust-growing, its culture the same as for other members of the *Odontoglossum* alliance.

FLOWER
8cm (3in) wide

FLOWER SPIKE
50cm (20in) long

PLANT
25cm (10in) high

POT SIZE
15cm (6in)

Kunthara Stefan Isler

Four popular genera have been combined to produce this richly coloured hybrid. The man-made genus, an older addition to the extensive *Odontoglossum* alliance registered in 1927, has been achieved by breeding with *Miltoniopsis*, *Cochlioda*, *Odontoglossum* and *Oncidium*, the result an eye-catching creation of reds and light reds. The *Miltoniopsis* has influenced the dramatic lip, while the *Cochlioda* gives the flower its rich colouring. The flower size has been slightly reduced by the *Oncidium* and the whole plant is compact enough for indoor growing. The blooms, with their vivid red sepals and petals, have a contrasting, fiddle-shaped orange lip. Carried on side branches to the main stem, they last several weeks and can be produced at almost any time of year.

FLOWER
4cm (1¹/₂in) wide

FLOWER SPIKE
100cm (40in) long

PLANT
18cm (7in) high

POT SIZE
15cm (6in)

Oncidium flexuosum

The yellow flowers of this Brazilian species introduced in 1821 are typical of many in the genus. The narrow petals and sepals, lightly barred with chestnut brown, are quite insignificant compared to the large, exaggerated deep yellow lip which flares out into a broad, flat surface. Given the fanciful name of 'dancing ladies', the lips resemble the swirling skirts of female figures as the orchids dance in a gentle wind. The small flowers are carried at the end of a long flower spike, on branches which give an attractive shower effect. The plant produces pseudobulbs at intervals, with a length of rhizome in between, enabling it to gain height for scrambling up a tree branch in its natural environment. In cultivation this makes keeping the plant in a pot hazardous, so it is better grown on a piece of cork bark, or in a pot in which a mossy pole has been inserted. When well-grown, many aerial roots are produced, which are an exciting part of the plant. The species blooms in autumn and lasts several weeks in flower.

GROWERS' TIP
Water less in winter, when the plant is resting.

FLOWER
2cm (1in) wide

FLOWER SPIKE
60cm (24in) long

PLANT
20cm (8in) high

POT SIZE
12cm (5in)

Oncidium Aloha Iwanaga

The *Oncidium* hybrids have become increasingly popular with the advent of further breeding which has given a much wider variety of colour and flower shapes. This yellow-flowered Hawaiian-bred hybrid can trace its ancestry back to three species, *O. flexuosum*, *O. sphacelatum* and *O. varicosum*, all a delightful yellow, with which it shares similarities of shape and structure, including the flared lip typical of the genus. These species, which originate from South and Central America, are seen less and less in cultivation but their legacy continues in the sparkling hybrids raised from them. This pretty hybrid produces tall flower spikes with modestly sized blooms on side branches along the stem. The petals and sepals are small and narrow, the yellow base dotted with chestnut brown towards their centres. These robust, large plants are mainly summer-flowering and will grow as well in a warmer temperature as in the recommended cooler temperatures.

FLOWER
5cm (2in) wide

FLOWER SPIKE
100cm (40in) long

PLANT
30cm (12in) high

POT SIZE
15cm (6in)

Brasscidium Kathleen Oka

This modern hybrid, raised in Hawaii in 1980, makes a large, robust plant with very large pseudobulbs and tall foliage. The flower spikes are also quite long, bearing numerous eye-catching blooms in a range of stunning colours. They appear from the mature pseudobulb at any time of the year and the blooms will last around four weeks. The plant is a cross between *Brassia*, creating the narrow petals and sepals, and *Oncidium*, bringing out the strong yellow colouring. This bigeneric hybrid is the result of the hybridizers' skill in producing an entirely new and unnatural hybrid. Its vigour and tolerance enable the plant to be grown in all climates, from temperate to tropical.

FLOWER
8cm (3in) wide

FLOWER SPIKE
70cm (28in) long

PLANT
35cm (14in) high

POT SIZE
18cm (7in)

Oncidium ornithorhynchum

This pretty species from Mexico and Guatemala is still widely grown today, making its mark among the larger, modern hybrids. First described in 1815, it did not come into general cultivation until some years later; a few hybrids have been made from it. The name *ornithorhynchum* derives from the Greek and means 'beak of a bird', a reference to the replica of a tiny dove's head which can clearly be seen at the centre of the bloom. It is notable for its strongly fragrant, rosy pink flowers, which are numerous on the compact flowering spikes, the individual blooms small and beautifully formed. The flowers appear in autumn at the end of the growing season, after which the plant has a brief rest. Similar to an *Odontoglossum*, this plant is smaller in stature but will readily produce more than one pseudobulb in a season.

Oncidium Sharry Baby 'Sweet Fragrance'

Yellow is the predominant colour among the oncidiums, but by no means all are yellow. This lovely Hawaiian-bred hybrid, raised along a different breeding line, has produced flowers which show the deep red colouring, accompanied by a strong chocolate fragrance, unusual among oncidiums, making this a popular plant for the amateur grower. The pretty, well-defined lip has the pinched middle and flared base found in *Oncidium ornithorhynchum* (see left) on one side of its parentage. The numerous flowers grow on side branches on the spike, which can be trained upright or allowed to arch naturally.

GROWERS' TIP
Grow with other odontoglossums and keep out of direct sun.

FLOWER
2cm (1in) wide

FLOWER SPIKE
20cm (8in) long

PLANT
20cm (8in) high

POT SIZE
8cm (3in)

FLOWER
2cm (1in) wide

FLOWER SPIKE
60cm (24in) long

PLANT
25cm (10in) high

POT SIZE
15cm (6in)

Miltoniopsis vexillaria 'Josephina'

Miltoniopsis vexillaria has had the greatest influence of all on the modern *Miltoniopsis* hybrids; it can be found in the background of almost every one, having been used extensively through several generations to produce today's showy clones. Brought into cultivation in 1872, it had been heard of since 1867, when it was described as *Odontoglossum vexillarium* and known as 'the scarlet odontoglossum'. The species is unique in its soft pastel colouring and its large, flat flowers on gently pendent sprays. It blooms in early summer, when its fragrant flowers will last up to three weeks. Today this is a collector's plant, prized for its natural beauty and maintained in specialist nurseries where it is still used for breeding. No longer wild-collected from its native Colombia for commercial distribution, those plants found in cultivation are propagations of stock plants that are many years old.

FLOWER
10cm (4in) wide

FLOWER SPIKE
23cm (9in) long

PLANT
30cm (12in) high

POT SIZE
10cm (4in)

Miltoniopsis St Helier 'Plum'

'Plum' is one of the colourful Jersey-bred St Helier orchids, illustrating the variation that can occur with the same hybrid, but different individual clones (see also 'Pink Delight', page 88). Raised in 1989, this is one of the very best clones, with the exquisite bold patterning at the centre of its flower. When a new hybrid is made the resulting seedlings will all flower differently, each having its own specific markings, some taking more after one parent than the other. Only the best clones are selected for mass propagation by meristem culture, which makes some of the finest orchids, such as this, available from different outlets across the world.

FLOWER
10cm (4in) wide

FLOWER SPIKE
23cm (9in) long

PLANT
30cm (12in) high

POT SIZE
10cm (4in)

Miltonia spectabilis

Closely related to the colourful miltoniopsis are the miltonias. The flowers are generally smaller and less flamboyant, although the resemblance is clearly seen in the dominant lip with attractive markings. One of the main differences, seen in this species introduced from Brazil in 1837, is that the miltonias produce a single bloom on a stem and lack the fragrance of *Miltoniopsis*. In fact, the miltoniopsis were once classified with the miltonias and all were known as miltonias. The botanical split separated the Colombian *Miltoniopsis* from the Brazilian *Miltonia* to create two distinct genera. Although closely related, these two genera will not breed together, which is surprising considering that *Miltoniopsis* will cross readily with other related genera such as *Odontoglossum*.

FLOWER
10cm (4in) wide

FLOWER SPIKE
10cm (4in) long

PLANT
15cm (6in) high

POT SIZE
10cm (4in)

Miltassia Cairns

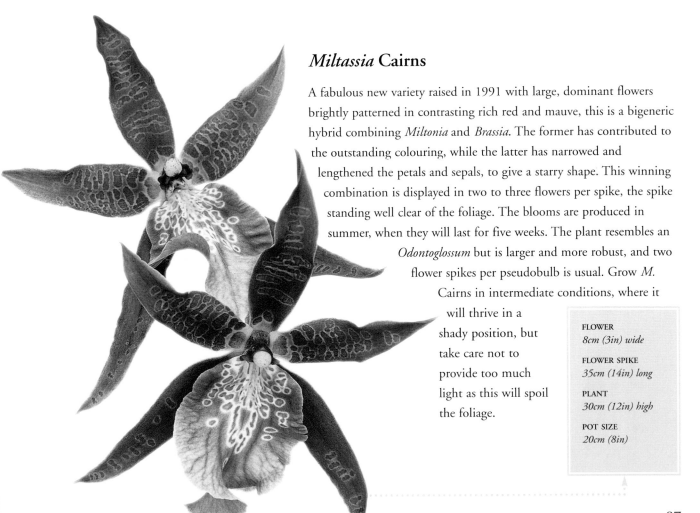

A fabulous new variety raised in 1991 with large, dominant flowers brightly patterned in contrasting rich red and mauve, this is a bigeneric hybrid combining *Miltonia* and *Brassia*. The former has contributed to the outstanding colouring, while the latter has narrowed and lengthened the petals and sepals, to give a starry shape. This winning combination is displayed in two to three flowers per spike, the spike standing well clear of the foliage. The blooms are produced in summer, when they will last for five weeks. The plant resembles an *Odontoglossum* but is larger and more robust, and two flower spikes per pseudobulb is usual. Grow *M.* Cairns in intermediate conditions, where it will thrive in a shady position, but take care not to provide too much light as this will spoil the foliage.

FLOWER
8cm (3in) wide

FLOWER SPIKE
35cm (14in) long

PLANT
30cm (12in) high

POT SIZE
20cm (8in)

Miltoniopsis St Helier 'Pink Delight'

This charming clone of St Helier is another example of the variation to be found in the Jersey-raised hybrids. It produces high-quality, long-lasting blooms at their best in spring, offering a combination of light, veined pink on the lip, dominated by the dark red butterfly-shaped mask at the centre; a broad white border separates the colours. This beautifully balanced flower was raised in Jersey by the Eric Young Orchid Foundation, among the world leaders in hybridizing this genus since the 1970s.

FLOWER
10cm (4in) wide

FLOWER SPIKE
23cm (9in) long

PLANT
30cm (12in) high

POT SIZE
10cm (4in)

Miltoniopsis Cindy Kane x Beethoven

The patterning on this highly individual flower has become subtle on the petals, with striking veining on the sepals. The lip carries the lovely 'waterfall' design which has been bred into several of the hybrids and can be traced back through many generations to the species *M. phalaenopsis*, with its highly patterned, teardrop lip. This patterning is much sought after and not always obtainable in such a defined manner as seen here. You could expect to pay more for hybrids with this decoration, which is seen mainly in the pink and red variations. This new hybrid has not yet been named, so it retains the parent names until registered in its own right.

FLOWER
10cm (4in) wide

FLOWER SPIKE
23cm (9in) long

PLANT
30cm (12in) high

POT SIZE
10cm (4in)

Miltoniopsis Mrs J B Crum 'Chelsea' FCC/RHS

There are many fine red hybrids available, but few illustrate the richness of this outstanding clone. The whole flower has a velvety appearance, enhanced by the white margin around the lip. This is an older hybrid raised in 1931 and bred from Lyceana 'Stampland' (see page 90); it received its first class certificate the following year. Water can spoil the blooms, so take care when watering these plants. Flowers produced during the main spring flowering season will be of a superior quality to those produced later in the autumn, though a second flowering is always welcome.

FLOWER
10cm (4in) wide

FLOWER SPIKE
23cm (9in) long

PLANT
30cm (12in) high

POT SIZE
10cm (4in)

Miltonia clowesii

Miltonia clowesii has the typical star-shaped flowers, with erect and pointed lateral petals and fiddle-shaped lip; spaced well apart on a tall, upright spike, they are richly coloured, waxy and fragrant. The main flowering season is summer and autumn. This species, cultivated since 1839, was found near Rio de Janeiro and sent to the Rev. John Clowes of Manchester, after whom it is named. The plant produces modest pseudobulbs with slender leaves, similar to an *Odontoglossum*.

GROWERS' TIP
Like many species, this plant shows off best when grown into a large specimen.

FLOWER
5cm (2in) wide

FLOWER SPIKE
60cm (24in) long

PLANT
30cm (12in) high

POT SIZE
15cm (6in)

Miltoniopsis Lyceana 'Stampland' FCC/RHS

This lovely two-coloured pansy orchid has the large lip, typical of the genus, which has become the most attractive part of the flower, especially when the central mask is well-defined and of a contrasting colour. It is an older hybrid, raised in Britain in 1925 by the famous odontoglossum specialists, Charlesworth & Co. of Haywards Heath in Surrey, England. This was a time when hundreds of similar crosses were being made, all from a very few species such as *M. vexillaria* and *M. roezlii*, from which came outstanding hybrids like Lyceana. The clone 'Stampland' was awarded its first class certificate in 1926, when it became the benchmark for future generations.

FLOWER
10cm (4in) wide

FLOWER SPIKE
23cm (9in) long

PLANT
30cm (12in) high

POT SIZE
10cm (4in)

Miltoniopsis Nancy Binks

The lip of this lovely hybrid shows an outstanding pattern, resembling a velvet cushion, at the centre of the flower, while the cherry red on the petals contrasts with the white background. This is a more recent hybrid, registered in 1985 and raised by an amateur grower, Dr Jim Binks – proof that the hobbyist can sometimes produce a hybrid to equal the successes of commercial nurseries. Allow the flower spikes to assume their natural arching habit, which is the best way to show the blooms off.

FLOWER
10cm (4in) wide

FLOWER SPIKE
23cm (9in) long

PLANT
30cm (12in) high

POT SIZE
10cm (4in)

FLOWER
10cm (4in) wide

FLOWER SPIKE
23cm (9in) long

PLANT
30cm (12in) high

POT SIZE
10cm (4in)

Miltoniopsis Eureka

This lovely, clear yellow *Miltoniopsis* points the way to a differently coloured range of hybrids, vying for attention with the rich reds and pinks. An outstanding hybrid with soft, buttery tones, Eureka is of American origin; raised in 1980, it is one of the latest in a successful line producing the elusive yellow colouring. Behind it lies Emotion, a salmon-pink hybrid which can be traced back to *M. vexillaria*; it produced one of the most notable yellows, the French-bred Alexander Dumas, which is in fact the parent of Eureka. With twice-yearly blooms from a modest-sized plant, it is an ideal first orchid, offering good rewards for a minimum of care. When in bloom, keep the flowers out of strong light to ensure they last as long as possible.

Miltoniopsis Zoro x Saffron Surprise

In this fine yellow flower of exceptional quality, a deep red-brown mask is combined with the two 'thumbprints' on the petals, enhancing the bloom and creating a further colour dimension. The yellow hybrids are extremely difficult to produce because yellow is not a prominent colour found among the species, and many will tone down to cream shortly after opening. By careful selective breeding, done mostly in the USA, using yellow-tinted forms of *M. vexillaria*, the hidden colour has been painstakingly extracted and will continue to be improved upon. Allow orchids like this to grow on to become specimen-sized, without dividing, for a number of years. A large plant with several new pseudobulbs flowering at once gives an impressive display and extends the period of bloom, as not all the flowers will be open at the same time.

FLOWER
10cm (4in) wide

FLOWER SPIKE
23cm (9in) long

PLANT
30cm (12in) high

POT SIZE
10cm (4in)

Miltoniopsis Robert Strauss 'White Flag'

Only a few of the top-quality hybrids have flowers of the purest white, as illustrated in this excellent clone in which the central markings of red and yellow set off the flower. Several clones of Robert Strauss have won awards, a testimony to the consistently high quality of this hybrid, raised in Britain in 1980. The outstanding quality of 'White Flag' is the roundness of its flamboyant lip, which is in perfect balance with the size of the petals and sepals. The adult plant carries four to six large blooms on a spike and it is normal for a well-grown plant to produce two flower spikes from each side of the pseudobulb at the same time.

FLOWER
10cm (4in) wide

FLOWER SPIKE
23cm (9in) long

PLANT
30cm (12in) high

POT SIZE
10cm (4in)

Coelogyne Memoria William Micholitz 'Burnham' AM/RHS

This wonderfully coloured clone with its glistening white petals and sepals and lip of almost solid gold is an outstanding cross in a genus which has produced very few hybrids of note. The plant has been raised from *C. mooreana* and *C. lawrenceana* and was named in honour of the German discoverer of both species, William Micholitz, a nineteenth-century plant hunter who introduced many new plants, including orchids, to the western world. This clone produces a large plant with sturdy, cone-shaped pseudobulbs and a pair of mid-green oval leaves. It blooms during spring and early summer, on a flower spike carrying up to six blooms.

FLOWER
9cm (3¹/₂in) wide
FLOWER SPIKE
30cm (12in) long
PLANT
45cm (18in) high
POT SIZE
18cm (7in)

Coelogyne barbata

This tall-growing Indian species became popular after about 1878 when the first living plants were sent from the Khasia Hills in northern India. It produces egg-shaped pseudobulbs topped by a pair of dark green, narrowly oval leaves, the flower spikes appearing from between the leaves as the pseudobulb develops. Once this has matured, the buds advance and the plant blooms in winter. The large, glistening white flowers have a contrasting dark brown bearded lip and a fringe of black hairs around the margin. The blooms open in succession along the stem, the first remaining fresh well after the last have opened. No longer wild-collected for export, this *Coelogyne* will readily grow from vegetative propagations.

GROWERS' TIP
Take care not to get water inside the funnel-shaped new growths.
FLOWER
5cm (2in) wide
FLOWER SPIKE
30cm (12 in) long
PLANT
30cm (12in) high
POT SIZE
18cm (7in)

Coelogyne mooreana 'Brockhurst' FCC/RHS

Coeogyne mooreana was discovered in Vietnam as late as 1906 and named after Mr F.W. Moore of the Glasnevin Botanic Gardens in Dublin. One of the biggest species in the genus, it produces spectacular, large, pristine white blooms with broad sepals and petals and a similar shaped lip, which carries a deep yellow stain at the centre. The clone 'Brockhurst', a superior form of the species, received its first class certificate the same year. The handsome plant has cone-shaped pseudo-bulbs with a pair of light green, narrow oval leaves; do not let the pseudobulbs shrivel. This strong, robust grower is equally at home in a greenhouse or light area indoors.

Coelogyne fuscescens

At the smaller end of the scale this pretty, dwarf-flowering *Coelogyne* species is an ideal windowsill orchid which will never outgrow its position. A native of India and Nepal, it was first described in 1830. The oval-shaped pseudobulbs carry two leaves, from between which the single flower is produced, buff-brown with a prettily marked lip. A large plant will be covered with blooms in autumn. When allowed to grow on *Coelogyne fuscescens* will form a dense mat of growths to cover its container. There are several similar, small species such as this one, and a group growing together makes an interesting feature.

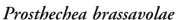

Prosthechea brassavolae

Among the prosthecheas is a group which carries spindly flowers on a flower spike from the apex of the elongated pseudobulb, one of the most colourful of which is *P. brassavolae*. This species has tall, slender pseudobulbs with two narrowly oval leaves, and originates from Central America, where it grows at high altitudes. The upright spike carries up to a dozen light green flowers, the oval-shaped lip being white, with the end tipped rosy mauve. The plant blooms during the summer months when the flowers will last for a long time. In a pot, the pseudobulbs may be well spread out and will quickly fill the surface space; it is better grown in a hanging wooden slatted basket which gives extra surface area with less compost underneath.

GROWERS' TIP
Grow in a hanging basket in a greenhouse or conservatory for best results.

FLOWER
4cm (1¹/₂in) wide

FLOWER SPIKE
25cm (10in) long

PLANT
30cm (12in) high

POT SIZE
15cm (6in)

Prosthechea Sunburst

This is one of only a very few hybrids which have been raised from the brightly coloured species, *P. vitellina* (see page 103), the other parent being the highly fragrant *P. radiata* (see page 103). The resulting cross, first raised by Mr E. Iwanaga of Hawaii in 1962, has given a plant with flowers which are midway between the two parents. Long-lasting and produced on an upright flower spike, they open a delicate shade of apricot and tone as they mature to creamy white.

FLOWER
3cm (1¹/₄in) wide

FLOWER SPIKE
15cm (6in) long

PLANT
15cm (6in) high

POT SIZE
10cm (4in)

Encyclia alata

This species comes mainly from Mexico and Honduras and is a low-altitude plant found at up to 1,000m (3,300ft) in forested areas. One of a group distinguished by their hard cone-shaped pseudobulbs, each of which has two or three long, leathery leaves. The long flower spike bears from a few to many flowers; though these are quite variable, the yellowish green petals and sepals are usually equal in size, and the decorative lip off-white, with some purple lines at the centre. The flowers are slightly fragrant and bloom between spring and autumn.

GROWERS' TIP
For optimum flowering, provide this species with good light.

FLOWER
2cm (1in) wide

FLOWER SPIKE
30cm (12in) long

PLANT
18cm (7in) high

POT SIZE
12cm (5in)

Prosthechea lancifolia

This pretty, highly fragrant Mexican species is one of several which have similar creamy white flowers with a cockleshell-shaped lip held at the top. The long sepals and petals hang loosely below the lip in a manner slightly reminiscent of the fully expanded fruiting body of an earth star fungus, found in winter in European woods and sandy places. The compact plant has short, club-shaped pseudobulbs and a pair of light green leaves; the upright flower spike comes from between the leaves.

This is an ideal species for the indoor home grower looking for compact plants with interesting flowers which will not take up too much room; it grows and flowers with great ease and is happy with minimal care.

FLOWER
2cm (1in) wide

FLOWER SPIKE
15cm (6in) long

PLANT
18cm (7in) high

POT SIZE
12cm (5in)

Prosthechea cochleata

A large number of prostheacheas produce their flowers with the lip at the top, in a position we would regard as upside down, as does this example. *P. cochleata* is known as the cockleshell orchid, a reference to its shell-like lip, and also as the octopus orchid, alluding to its long, drooping, ribbon-like petals. This species was the first tropical epiphytic orchid to bloom in Britain, which it did at the Royal Botanic Gardens in Kew in 1763. The green and black flowers come from the top of the club-shaped pseudobulb in a succession lasting weeks or months depending on plant size. This is a great orchid for the beginner, as it starts flowering on a very young plant, then gives unlimited exotic-looking flowers; on reaching maturity, it becomes perpetually blooming.

FLOWER
3cm (1¼in) wide

FLOWER SPIKE
15cm (6in) long

PLANT
30cm (12in) high

POT SIZE
12cm (5in)

Prosthechea radiata

This is another delightful *Prosthechea* to grow. The plant produces slender pseudobulbs with a pair of mid-green leaves; the upright flower spike comes from the top of the pseudobulb and carries up to a dozen cheery little blooms. These have a strong fragrance, and on a large plant the scent will fill a room. Found in Guatemala, Honduras and Mexico, this plant is easily grown on to become specimen size as it rarely drops its foliage and will remain looking good for many years without needing to be divided (unless this is to increase the number of plants). The plant blooms during summer and lasts for a long time in flower.

GROWERS' TIP
Keep water droplets away from the blooms as they can cause premature spotting.

FLOWER
2cm (1in) wide

FLOWER SPIKE
10cm (4in) long

PLANT
18cm (7in) high

POT SIZE
12cm (5in)

Prosthechea vitellina

Unusual among the prosthecheas is this species unique in the genus for its bright, vermilion-red flowers. The sepals and petals are oval and equally presented and the small, duckbill-shaped lip is orange. The flower spike is usually held upright above the plant and carries up to a dozen flowers, blooming in late summer and autumn. The plant originates from Mexico and was first described in 1833. It remains popular among enthusiasts, though very little hybridizing has been done with this species, and the few hybrids raised have not retained the vivid colouring which makes it so highly desirable.

FLOWER
2cm (1in) wide

FLOWER SPIKE
10cm (4in) long

PLANT
15cm (6in) high

POT SIZE
8cm (3in)

Dendrobium infundibulum

This beautiful species, introduced from Burma in 1859, produces a handsome plant with tall canes densely covered in fine black hairs. The buds, which emerge in early spring at the start of the plant's growing season, are also protected by black-haired bracts. The flowers appear in threes or fours on stems opposite each leaf axil along the whole length of the cane, each large bloom a delicate papery white with a golden yellow highlight at the centre of the lip. This species varies in shape from well-rounded flowers to the more spread-out bloom seen here. This is one of the easiest dendrobiums to grow and flower to perfection, provided it is given plenty of water and light, moist conditions in the summer growing months. Although the newest pseudobulbs (canes) produce the flowers, older ones will often give a secondary blooming from nodes at the tip of already-flowered canes. Species from this group will not breed with *D. nobile* types.

FLOWER
10cm (4in) wide

PLANT
45cm (18in) high

POT SIZE
12cm (5in)

Dendrobium senile

Dendrobium senile (below) is a pretty dwarf species from Thailand. The elongated pseudobulbs (canes) are covered in dense white hairs, forming a protective layer. The waxy flowers, produced in ones and twos on a short stem from the leaf axils, are fragrant and last over several weeks during the spring months. This species has bright yellow flowers with a green centre to the lip, their shape typical of many dendrobiums from India and the Far East. The leaves are usually shed after one or two years and the plant can become completely leafless during the winter rest.

GROWERS' TIP
Keep this orchid dry and in full light during its resting period.

FLOWER
4cm (1½ in) wide

PLANT
10cm (4in) high

POT SIZE
5cm (2in)

Dendrobium Superstar Champion

This highly decorative flower is a modern-day *D. nobile* type of hybrid. The plants are a manageable size as their pseudobulbs, or canes, are stout and shortened rather than being long and thin as they are in most of the species. The plants grow well during the summer growing season, making up their canes in a few months. They rest in winter, when they need little or no watering; water only if the pseudobulbs shrivel. The spring will be welcomed by an explosion of buds along the length of the newest cane, and the flowers will entirely cover the plant. Colours can vary from white, through yellow and pink to the deeper shades of red-mauve, with contrasting lip decorations.

FLOWER
6cm (2½in) wide

PLANT
45cm (18in) high

POT SIZE
15cm (6in)

Dendrobium Oriental Paradise

The group of hybrids on these pages have all been raised from the species *Dendrobium nobile*, and are often referred to as '*D. nobile*-type' hybrids. They exhibit the large, rounded flowers with a circular lip of equal proportions. The range of colours among pink, mauve, yellow and white shades is almost endless, each hybrid possessing its own unique lip coloration and central highlight. Because of the infinite variations in colour, it is best to look for these plants in flower in the spring to ensure you select the colouring you like best. With so many to choose from, a collection can be made from just this type of *Dendrobium* hybrid alone, without having to repeat any colour.

FLOWER
6cm (2¹/₂in) wide

PLANT
45cm (18in) high

POT SIZE
15cm (6in)

Dendrobium Lucky Seven

Another delightful *D. nobile*-type hybrid, this orchid illustrates the depth of colour which can be achieved by selective breeding to bring out its potential richness. The centre of the lip is enlivened with an almost black disc which attracts the pollinating insect. These lovely flowers, produced in the spring, have a fuller shape, with more rounded petals and sepals than is apparent in the species; their size has also been increased with selective breeding over several generations. Although bred from species which include some that are deciduous, the hybrids tend to remain evergreen, shedding only a few leaves at a time from the older canes, which then assume a supporting role to the rest of the plant. The older, flowered and leafless canes can be used for propagating by severing them from the main plant, cutting them into pieces with a node in the centre and potting them up in a community pot (see page 217).

FLOWER
6cm (2¹/₂in) wide

PLANT
45cm (18in) high

POT SIZE
15cm (6in)

Dendrobium nobile var. *cooksonii*

In this colourful variety of *D. nobile*, the flower exhibits the rose-pink colouring of the type, but also carries a replica pattern of the lip marking on the lateral petals. Uncommon but not unknown in orchids, this is called peloria and can take several forms, such as the lip repeating the appearance of the petals and being devoid of any other adornment. In some instances, this attractive mutation is encouraged to breed into further generations, with limited success. This horticultural variant appeared among a consignment of *D. nobile*, and was grown in the collection of Norman C. Cookson, a noted grower who exhibited it for the first time around 1885. All plants now in cultivation are propagated divisions of this one plant. This *Dendrobium* is capable of flowering the entire length of its newest canes, but flowering to such perfection takes skill. During the winter the plant needs a dry rest; if watering is started too early in the year, before the flower buds are fully developed, they will turn into adventitious growths instead.

FLOWER
5cm (2in) wide

PLANT
45cm (18in) high

POT SIZE
15cm (6in)

Dendrobium Tancho Queen

One further example of the colour variations found among the hybrids from *D.nobile*. This latest hybrid illustrates the stunning combination of plain white petals and sepals with the deep crimson-black centre to the lip. The flowers are produced from short stems which arise from the nodes along the side of the newest pseudobulbs, which are the tall canes developed each year as the plant progresses with its new growth. While they need to be grown in small pots because of their fine rooting system, the plants can become top heavy, especially when they carry the extra weight of flowers. Stand the plants in a larger, heavier container which has a drainage hole at the base to prevent the plant falling over.

FLOWER
6cm (2¹/₂in) wide

PLANT
45cm (18in) high

POT SIZE
15cm (6in)

Dendrochilum magnum

This autumn-flowering, cool-growing species needs water all year and is one of a number from Malaya and the Philippine Islands. Those with white flowers are known as the silver chain orchids; this species with light yellow flowers is called a golden chain orchid. The flowers are carried on a long, slender, drooping flower spike that arises from the base of the new growth and blooms for around three weeks in early autumn. Up to eighty flowers are closely packed in two rows along the spike; in some species the inflorescence is twisted through its length. The flowers are strongly fragrant, and a large plant can produce numerous spikes. The pseudobulbs are small, supporting a single leaf. All the species are extremely popular and worth collecting. The genus was first described in 1825.

GROWERS' TIP
Too much water lying on the foliage can cause premature spotting.

FLOWER
1cm (¹/₂in) wide

FLOWER SPIKE
75cm (30in) long

PLANT
30cm (12in) high

POT SIZE
8cm (3in)

Pleione speciosa

This species, in cultivation since 1914, is undoubtedly one of the richest-coloured in this much-loved genus of small plants. The flowers are typically bright magenta, although intensity of colour can vary. Originally just one clone of the species was known but more plants were later obtained from its native China. The plant has proved to be extremely good for breeding and has produced a number of fine quality hybrids in brilliant hues, greatly widening the appeal of these popular windowsill gems. *P. speciosa* is typical of the genus with its widespread petals and sepals and generously coloured lip, gaily patterned with yellow striations and red dots. A single flower is usually produced but occasionally two will open on the stem; the blooms last for about ten days.

FLOWER
6cm (2¹/₂in) wide

FLOWER SPIKE
10-15cm (4-6in) long

PLANT
12cm (5in) high

PAN SIZE
5cm (2in)

Pleione Shantung 'Ridgeway' AM/RHS

This beautiful apricot-coloured hybrid is the result of crossing two species, the well-known *P. formosana*, which has pink and white forms, with the lesser-known *P. confusa*, the only yellow species in the genus. Originally known as *P. forrestii*, this latter species was collected in south-west China in 1904 by the plant collector George Forrest. Until recently only a single clone was in cultivation and this was proving difficult to grow and breed. But in the late 1970s further clones were bred and the breeding qualities of the species were realised with the raising of such hybrids as Shantung, produced in 1977. The rich yellow of this species has been combined with a pink form of *P. formosana* to produce Shantung's lovely apricot colouring.

FLOWER
8cm (3in) wide

FLOWER SPIKE
15-20cm (4-6in) long

PLANT
15cm (6in) high

PAN SIZE
10cm (4in)

Pleione Etna

This is a primary hybrid, raised in Britain in 1979 from the Chinese species, *P. speciosa* and *P. limprichtii*, which are closely related and look similar. Etna therefore shows little difference from the species but has inherited vigour while retaining gloriously bright colouring. This hybrid is also important for the genus because both species are available from very few clones and this further breeding has enabled nurseries to bring a much wider range into cultivation. The flower is slightly smaller than that of *P. speciosa* and resembles its other parent in this respect. Etna makes a perfect 'first orchid' and a single pseudobulb will multiply rapidly to provide a whole panful within a few years. *P. limprichtii*, in cultivation since 1934, is covered with snow in the wild during the coldest part of the year.

FLOWER
6cm (2¹/₂in) wide

FLOWER SPIKE
10-15cm (4-6in) long

PLANT
12cm (5in) high

PAN SIZE
5cm (2in)

Pleione formosana var. *semi-alba*

This is probably the best known of the species and among the easiest to grow; in sheltered areas it can be raised outdoors in a specially prepared bed. The species is similar to *P. speciosa* and many hybrids have been produced with one or both as a starting point. Because *P. formosana* is extremely variable, with many colour variations, carefully selective breeding has enabled a wide range of colours to be produced among its hybrids. While the best clones command high prices, the more ordinary ones are still desirable; it can often be found in outlets other than specialist nurseries, sold unpotted and unestablished. This *Pleione* has glistening white sepals and petals, with discreet yellow and brown lip colouring. A pure white variety is also found, which is devoid of colouring on the lip. It is not unusual for this plant to produce two flowers on a stem.

GROWERS' TIP
Bury this orchid's fast-growing new roots carefully to prevent them pushing out of the compost.

FLOWER
6cm (2¹/₂in) wide

FLOWER SPIKE
10-15cm (4-6in) long

PLANT
12cm (5in) high

PAN SIZE
5cm (2in)

Brassia Arania Verde

The brassias are the well-known spider orchids, so called for their extraordinarily long, thin petals and sepals which are held out stiffly. The lip is large by comparison, but also narrow and pointed. The flowers are extremely fragrant, and are produced in long sprays of up to ten blooms. They are largely green, as seen here, with rich chocolate-brown barring along the petals and sepals. The plant resembles an *Odontoglossum*, with which genus it will interbreed, and has robust pseudobulbs and two broadly oval leaves. The flower spikes appear in late spring as the pseudobulbs mature, and the blooms will last for five to six weeks. This hybrid was raised in 1990.

FLOWER
25cm (10in) long

FLOWER SPIKE
60cm (24in) long

PLANT
50cm (20in) high

POT SIZE
18cm (7in)

Brassia verrucosa

Brassias, known as spider orchids for their amazingly long, narrow petals and sepals, are exciting orchids to grow. Tolerating a temperature range of 10°C (50°F) minimum to 30°C maximum (85°F), this South American epiphytic species is the most prized in the genus for its light green sprays of delightfully fragrant flowers, which may be up to six or eight on a stem. The plants resemble robust odontoglossums, to which they are closely related, and with which they will interbreed in certain combinations. In multi-generic hybrids, however, the length of the flower parts is never so great, and much of the original charm of this species is lost. The flowers appear in early summer and last for about three weeks.

FLOWER
20cm (8in) long

FLOWER SPIKE
30cm (12in) long

PLANT
20cm (8in) high

POT SIZE
15cm (6in)

Brassia Rex

Though not a large genus, the brassias are represented in many mixed collections by a few of the species and their hybrids, such as Rex. They are probably most distinctive and easily recognizable by their spider-like flowers which produce extremely long and narrow petals and sepals. In this hybrid the sepals and petals have been further extended, with bold brown patterning on the green base. The lip, also elongated, is white to creamy white and decorated with some brown dotting. These sweetly scented flowers are produced on long, arching flower spikes in early summer. The plants are neat growers, resembling the odontoglossums with which they will readily interbreed. Position these plants in light shade in summer and full light in winter.

FLOWER
15cm (6in) long

FLOWER SPIKE
30cm (12in) long

PLANT
25cm (10in) high

POT SIZE
18cm (7in)

Trichopilia tortilis

Grows in the tropical rainforests of South America. The neat plants, with oval pseudobulbs and a single leaf, produce one or two dramatic flowers on a slender spike in spring or early summer. The long, narrow petals and sepals twist along their length to give these plants their common name of 'corkscrew orchid'. The lip is closed at the top but flares out dramatically to a circular white globe with a deep yellow centre. This is an easy orchid to grow in pots or mounted on cork bark.

FLOWER
10cm (4in) wide

PLANT
15cm (6in) high

POT SIZE
8cm (3in)

Anguloa uniflora

The anguloas are a small genus known as the cradle orchids because of their loosely hinged lip at the centre of the cupped bloom, which rocks back and forth when the flower is moved from side to side. The other common name is tulip orchid, a reference to its cupped or tulip shape. This species comes from South America; it was discovered in Peru in 1798 and grows at high altitudes in the Andes; it first flowered in cultivation in 1842. The tall, robust plants produce oval pseudobulbs with several wide, ribbed leaves, shed for the winter when the plant is dormant. Activity starts in the spring, the new growths developing alongside the flower spike, which terminates in a single white bloom whose large petals and sepals are peppered on the inside with deep pink. The plant benefits from being shaded lightly in summer, with a mature specimen producing multiple flowers in one season. The anguloas are related to the lycastes, with which they will interbreed to produce a bigeneric hybrid genus, *Angulocaste*, that includes some of the largest flowers among the popular orchids.

GROWERS' TIP
This plant benefits from being watered well in summer, and kept dry in winter.

FLOWER
5cm (2in) wide

PLANT
50cm (20in) high

POT SIZE
15cm (6in)

Masdevallia Whiskers

These charming, mysterious little orchids are among the greatest characters in the orchid family. The neat, epiphytic plants have tufted stems and solitary leaves, produced from a short stem at the base of the plant, from where the flower spike emerges. Their triangular-shaped flowers, which may be single or several on a stem, are made up from grossly enlarged and partially fused sepals, often with long tails. The insignificant petals and lip are hidden away at the centre of the bloom. Their distinctive shape has earned them the common name of kite orchids. Masdevallias like to be kept evenly moist all year round, never getting too wet at the roots. Their flowering time is various but mainly during the summer months. The numerous and varied species within the genus come from a wide area of tropical South America, many making their home in the Peruvian Andes. Among the hybrids there is a huge variety of colours, shapes and sizes of flower. This striking hybrid has come from the most flamboyant of the species, *M. veitchiana*, which it resembles in its vibrant orange-red colouring. Shade well in summer, less in winter and keep within a temperature range of 10°C (50°F) minimum to 24°C (75°F) maximum.

FLOWER
4cm (1¹/₂in) wide

PLANT
15cm (6in) high

POT SIZE
10cm (4in)

Stanhopea maculosa

The stanhopeas are truly amazing orchids, widely distributed throughout South and Central America where they grow epiphytically on stout branches in forest areas. Their large, ribbed pseudobulbs are topped by a single thick, leathery leaf but their most unusual feature is that they produce their large, fleshy flowers on spikes which hang below the plant, or which burrow down through the compost to emerge underneath. For this reason they are always grown in hanging baskets, either open, slatted wooden types, or plastic aquatic net pots, which enables the flower spike to push out through the bottom of the container. The spikes emerge in summer (when the plant should be well watered if in growth) and carry some of the most curiously shaped of all orchid flowers: these are richly coloured and highly fragrant but last for three to four days only. The base of the lip carries two horn-like projections which assist the pollinating insect to enter the flower at the right angle. These have given this orchid its common name of bull's horns orchid, or Toro, Toro! – the large red splashes on the petals are said to be the blood of the bull. The curious flowers need to be viewed sideways to discern the unique shape of their petals, sepals and lip.

GROWERS' TIP
These plants benefit from light shade in summer and full light in winter.

FLOWER
8cm (3in) wide

FLOWER SPIKE
23-30cm (9-12in) long

PLANT
20cm (8in) high

BASKET SIZE
12cm (5in)

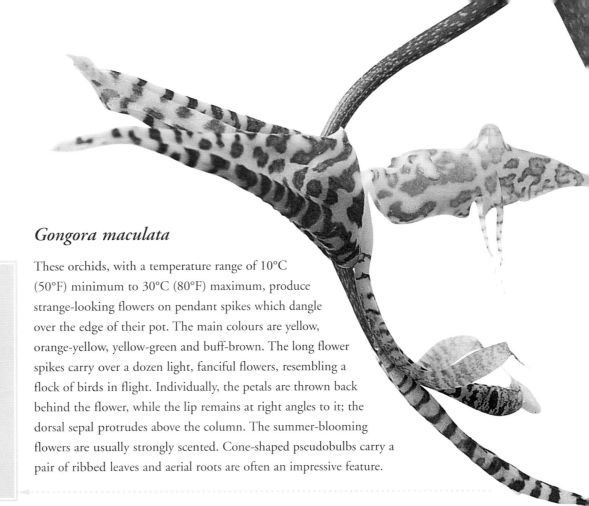

Gongora maculata

These orchids, with a temperature range of 10°C (50°F) minimum to 30°C (80°F) maximum, produce strange-looking flowers on pendant spikes which dangle over the edge of their pot. The main colours are yellow, orange-yellow, yellow-green and buff-brown. The long flower spikes carry over a dozen light, fanciful flowers, resembling a flock of birds in flight. Individually, the petals are thrown back behind the flower, while the lip remains at right angles to it; the dorsal sepal protrudes above the column. The summer-blooming flowers are usually strongly scented. Cone-shaped pseudobulbs carry a pair of ribbed leaves and aerial roots are often an impressive feature.

GROWERS' TIP
Shade lightly and water well in summer for the best results.

FLOWER
4cm (1¹/₂in) wide

FLOWER SPIKE
30cm (12in) long

PLANT
20cm (8in) high

BASKET SIZE
12cm (5in)

Gongora galeata

This is one of the smaller-growing species within an extraordinary genus. Introduced around 1830 from Mexico, it underwent several name changes before being included in this genus in 1854. The attractive plants have ribbed, cone-shaped pseudobulbs with a pair of mid-green leaves. The slender, wire-like pendant flower spikes produce several orange-scented flowers during the summer, ranging in colour from yellow-green to buff-brown. In times past many more gongoras were grown, but today the species are rarely seen. With very little hybridizing having been done between them, only a few gongoras remain in cultivation.

GROWERS' TIP
The cultivation needs for this orchid are the same as for G.maculata (above).

FLOWER
4cm (1¹/₂in) wide

FLOWER SPIKE
15cm (6in) long

PLANT
20cm (8in) high

BASKET SIZE
12cm (5in)

Lycaste skinneri

This species was introduced from Guatemala in 1840 by George ure-Skinner, after whom it was named. Today, it is the national flower of that country. This is an extremely pretty and variable species which was once grown extensively in collections, and the many colour forms were all collected. Today it is very rare, and it is the colourful hybrids which have been produced from it that are more often seen. The species is usually encountered under the above name, although botanically it is described as *L. virginalis*. The plant is semi-deciduous and enjoys cool conditions. One flower per spike appears in spring and will last for six weeks.

GROWERS' TIP
Water plentifully in summer and rest dry in winter for best results.

FLOWER
10cm (4in) wide

FLOWER SPIKE
20cm (8in) long

PLANT
45cm (18in) high

POT SIZE
10cm (4in)

Thunia marshalliana

Thunias are great fun to grow. This popular species is one of no more than six in a tiny genus native to India, China and South-East Asia. They produce tall, fleshy canes (or pseudobulbs), leafed along their length with soft-textured, narrowly oval leaves. They start their new growth in early spring and grow at a fast rate through the summer (when they should be shaded and watered well), flowering from the top of the completed cane to produce a cascading spray of foaming flowers. The blooms, produced in short succession and lasting weeks at a time, have pure white petals and sepals, their deeply frilled and hairy lip overlaid with golden yellow. After flowering, the canes mature and all the foliage is shed. In winter the canes can be left in their pots, or taken out and placed in trays. After repotting, the old canes will shrivel and die.

GROWERS' TIP
Pot up early in the new year, when new growth is seen at the base.

FLOWER
20cm (4in) wide

PLANT
60cm (24in) high

POT SIZE
15cm (6in)

Bulbophyllum elassonotum

Belonging to the largest genus of orchids, this pretty plant carries its small, neat yellow flowers in a dense raceme reminiscent of a fir cone. Its pungent scent suggests pollination by fruit flies. Its origins are somewhat obscure, but it holds a place among the smaller-growing, small-flowered collectables and is desirable for its relative ease of growing. It produces small, rounded pseudobulbs with a single leaf and densely packed flowers that last two to three weeks in early spring. This orchid will grow in a small pot under cool conditions, or it can be grown on a piece of cork bark which, if left alone for many years, it will cover with a solid ball of pseudobulbs and leaves.

FLOWER
1cm (1/2in) long

PLANT
15cm (6in) high

POT SIZE
10cm (4in)

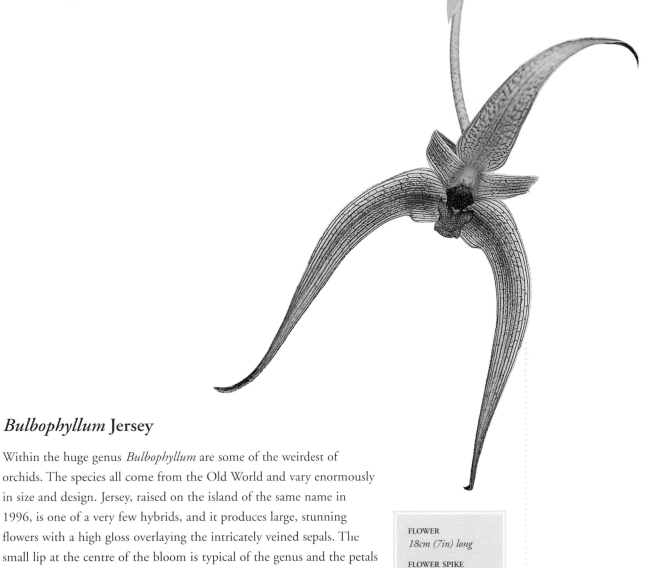

Bulbophyllum Jersey

Within the huge genus *Bulbophyllum* are some of the weirdest of orchids. The species all come from the Old World and vary enormously in size and design. Jersey, raised on the island of the same name in 1996, is one of a very few hybrids, and it produces large, stunning flowers with a high gloss overlaying the intricately veined sepals. The small lip at the centre of the bloom is typical of the genus and the petals are neatly folded back. The flowers are carried singly on drooping flower spikes throughout summer, and they will last for about three weeks. The plant produces rounded pseudobulbs with a single thick leaf. It is fairly easy to grow but take care not to overwater in winter while it is at rest.

FLOWER
18cm (7in) long

FLOWER SPIKE
25cm (10in) long

PLANT
25cm (10in) high

POT SIZE
15cm (6in)

Intermediate orchids

Wherever you can offer a few extra degrees of heat in winter, a whole
new range of orchids opens up. Intermediate-growing orchids need
temperatures ranging from a minimum of 13°C (55°F) on winter nights
to a summer daytime maximum of 30°C (85°F). A number of them
will grow alongside the cool-growing orchids for most of the year, but
they need the extra warmth on winter nights. By making only small
adjustments to a growing area, you should be able to create a suitable
environment for the warmer types: a few extra degrees at night can
easily be achieved by moving them to a room in the house which is
naturally warmer, or where you maintain a little background heating
overnight. Another possibility is to divide off a section of greenhouse
where there is enough room, without creating too confining a division.
Separating cool-growing orchids from intermediates during the winter
ensures that both groups are grown in a temperature range that suits
them, while keeping them together in the hope that all will thrive will
result in some doing much better than others. Cool-growing orchids
kept warmer at night to suit the intermediates may not bloom as they
need the night-time drop of a few degrees to initiate flowering. Keep a
maximum–minimum thermometer in each of the different growing
areas, to be sure of giving your orchids the temperature range they need.

Sophrocattleya Rocket Burst 'Deep Enamel' AM/RHS

Among the *Cattleya* alliance is the genus *Sophronitis*. The best of these produces a small, vivid red flower and the whole plant is less than 15cm (6in) in bloom. When the red species *S. coccinea* is crossed with a larger, small-flowered *Sophronitis* or *Cattleya*, the result is deep coloured hybrids such as Rocket Burst, awarded on both sides of the Atlantic for its exquisitely vibrant colouring and star-shaped flowers. It blooms in spring and lasts for up to four weeks.

FLOWER
5cm (2in) wide

PLANT
30cm (12in) high

POT SIZE
15cm (6 in)

Sophronitis Pulcherrima

This is a modern version of a much older cross first made over 100 years ago between two Brazilian species, *Sophronitis purpurata* (introduced in 1852 and still very popular in collections) and the lesser-known but equally attractive *S. lobata*. Today's hybrid looks considerably different to the 1898 cross, because other clones of the species have been used, creating a distinct and beautiful new hybrid which retains the original name. The wide flower has the typical open shape associated with many sophronitis, an extremely variable genus, while the lip is distinctly trumpet-shaped, flared at the end and richly coloured. The pseudobulbs are long and slender with a solitary leaf.

FLOWER
18cm (7in) wide

PLANT
60cm (24in) high

POT SIZE
20cm (8in)

Sophrocattleya Drumbeat

This bigeneric hybrid genus is the result of a combination of *Sophronitis* and *Cattleya*, first made in 1887. Many such crosses have been made over the years, producing fine, large-flowered varieties that display lush colourings on showy blooms which may be white, yellow or shades of lavender-pink or purple. Some of these hybrids are spring-blooming, while others produce their flowers in autumn; hybrids may take their flowering cue from one parent or the other. The delightful fragrance is maintained in hybridization in this alliance, and in some hybrids is even enhanced. This well-rounded, frilled bloom is the result of selective breeding to combine various outstanding qualities.

FLOWER
15cm (6in) wide

PLANT
38cm (15in) high

POT SIZE
15cm (6in)

Sophrocattleya Veldorado 'Polka' AM/RHS

The diversity of flower colour is well illustrated in this superb, French-bred modern *Cattleya* hybrid, raised in 1976 from Amber Glow and Colibri. One to three flowers can be produced on the spike, the rich yellow petals and sepals contrasting vividly with the deep ruby lip, shot through with gold veining towards the throat. The blooms also carry a sweet fragrance. This medium-sized plant has a single, semi-rigid leaf and blooms once a year when the season's pseudobulb is completed; the usual flowering time is autumn. To encourage the flowers to live longer, place out of strong light while in bloom and keep on the dry side.

FLOWER
12cm (5in) wide

PLANT
38cm (15in) high

POT SIZE
15cm (6in)

Sophrocattleya Elizabeth Fulton 'La Tuilerie' AM/RHS

Raised in 1977 in the USA from Amber Glen and the Brazilian species *Cattleya bicolor*, this richly coloured clone is the result of generations of selective breeding to bring out all the qualities exhibited in its flower. The coppery colouring, rarely seen among cattleyas, is a welcome addition to an already extensive colour range. The sepals and petals display the ideal shape looked for in this genus and the exquisitely self-coloured lip is a perfect complement to them. The plant is a neat grower, its slender pseudobulbs carrying a single leaf, with the blooms appearing well above the foliage. One to three flowers may be expected, the usual number being two, and these appear in autumn.

FLOWER
12cm (5in) wide

PLANT
38cm (15in) high

POT SIZE
15cm (6in)

Cattleya Little Miss Charming

Raised along a different breeding line from *C. Hawaiian Wedding Song* (right) this attractive hybrid is an example of the variety to be found among *Cattleya*. Here the flower is spaced out, the petals and sepals narrower and neither touching nor overlapping as in the rounder flowers. Two to three blooms are produced on a longer stem, while the pseudobulbs are tall and slender with a single long, oval leaf.

The parents of this American-raised hybrid, registered in 1984, are Snowberry and the species, *C. loddigesii*. Since Snowberry already has this species as one of its parents, the dominant genes are from *C. loddigesii*, as can be seen in both the flower shape and growth habit of Little Miss Charming.

FLOWER
10cm (4in) wide

PLANT
30cm (12in) high

POT SIZE
15cm (6in)

Cattlianthe Sir Jeremiah Colman

In the search for the elusive blue in cattleyas, this plant is supreme. An older hybrid which still retains its classic status, it was raised in the USA in 1976 and named in honour of Sir Jeremiah Colman, an eminent breeder of blue-flowered *Cattleya* hybrids during the first half of the twentieth century. The blue colouring is obtained from the *coerulea* form of several *Cattleya* and *Guarianthe* species and this plant has proved to be an excellent breeder, producing further blue cattleyas over the years. Its sepals and petals are light, eggshell blue, the frilled lip mauve around the edge and yellow at the centre. A neat grower, its slender pseudobulbs have a pair of narrow, oval leaves at the apex.

FLOWER
9cm (3¹/₂in) wide

PLANT
30cm (12in) high

POT SIZE
12cm (5in)

Cattleya Hawaiian Wedding Song

In this American-raised white hybrid, which is pure *Cattleya*, the petals have become so frilled and enlarged that their shape is almost undefined, causing the flower to lose some of the roundness that is the hallmark of quality among these lovely hybrids. The lip is well defined, however, and exhibits a perfectly frilled edge and deep yellow throat. This modern hybrid is from the unifoliate group, producing one leathery oval leaf, and was registered in 1982 from the parents Angel Bells and Claesiana, in Hawaii. Angel Bells comes from Empress Bells and Little Angel, raised in 1960 from the famous stud plant Bow Bells, while Claesiana is an older, English-bred primary hybrid raised in 1916 from the species *C. intermedia* and *C. loddigesii*.

FLOWER
12cm (5in) wide

PLANT
38cm (15in) high

POT SIZE
15cm (6in)

Sophrocattleya Persepolis

The parents of this 1973-registered bigeneric hybrid are *Cattleya* Kitiwake and *Sophronitis* Pegi Mayne; it was raised in the USA from a line of similar crosses. The lip shows a marked *Cattleya* influence and with its rich magenta colouring provides an ideal contrast for this winning colour combination. This is an important breeding plant which has gone on to produce mainly summer-blooming white-flowered hybrids. The plant is strong and robust with a thick, leathery leaf. In winter these orchids like all the light available, but early spring sunshine can quickly burn through their tender leaf structures, so they should always be given some shade, or moved to a shadier place, from spring onwards, once the sun starts to gain power.

FLOWER
15cm (6in) wide

PLANT
38cm (15in) high

POT SIZE
15cm (6in)

Catyclia El Hatillo 'Santa Maria'

This American-raised clone combines the qualities of two genera to produce an endearing flower. It is a primary hybrid from *Cattleya mossiae* and *Encyclia tampensis*, the former being an earlier introduction from Venezeula, described in 1836. It first flowered in the collection of Mrs Moss in 1838 and today can be found in most, if not all, modern *Cattleya* hybrids. In this cross the *Encyclia* has proved to be the dominant parent, influencing the overall flower shape, while the vivid lip colouring is typical of many cattleyas. The neat-growing plant has slender, elongated pseudobulbs supporting a pair of narrow, rigid leaves, from between which the flower spike emerges. This grows upright and carries four to five fragrant flowers, coloured a light creamy green with a brightly contrasting lip. The plant likes to be warm and provided with good light all year.

FLOWER
5cm (2in) wide

PLANT
20cm (8in) high

POT SIZE
12cm (5in)

Cattleychea Siam Jade

The prostheccheas are a genus closely related to the cattleyas and help to make up the *Cattleya* alliance. When selected *Prosthechea mariae* is crossed with cattleyas some startlingly different coloured plants emerge, as with this beautiful clear green American-bred hybrid. The sepals and petals are more thickly textured than those of other cattleyas and the attractive cream lip is almost rigid. This plant is small and compact, the pseudobulbs being shortened; its flowering season is various, the flowers blooming most often in spring.

FLOWER
5cm (2in) wide

PLANT
10cm (4in) high

POT SIZE
10cm (4in)

Dendrobium goldschmidtianum

A pretty species from the Philippines, *D. goldschmidtianum* produces long, pendant canes which are leafed along their length; it retains some foliage throughout the year. The attractive rosy-mauve flowers are produced from side nodes along the canes and appear in a drooping truss of clustered blooms in spring, following a dry winter's rest period. When these canes have matured good light is an important factor in ensuring a show of flowers. This species was quite rare in cultivation until recent years when it became more readily available from nursery-raised stock. It blooms and re-blooms from the older, leafless canes. It is best grown in a hanging basket, close to the glass.

GROWERS' TIP
Spray well and keep moist during the summer while the long canes are developing.

FLOWER
1cm (¹/2in) wide

PLANT
30cm (12in) high

POT SIZE
12cm (5in)

Dendrobium victoria-regina

This species is closely related to *D. goldschmidtianum* (see right) which it resembles in habit; both species come from the Philippines and grow on trees as epiphytes. *D. victoria-regina*, 30cm (12in) high, produces slender canes that become deciduous after two to three years. As the canes mature they assume a pendant position, which is why they are best cultivated in 7-cm (3-in) pots or small baskets suspended above the staging, where their natural habit can be allowed to develop. Alternatively, the canes may be tied into an upright position, which does not affect the plants or their flowering. The small, bluish-mauve flowers only 2cm (1in) wide, are produced in clusters of two or three from midway to the top of the canes; several canes can flower in one season. Good light is necessary to prompt flowering in the spring, but also at other times of year.

GROWERS' TIP
This species can tolerate a minimum temperature of 10°C (50°F).

FLOWER
15cm (6in) wide

PLANT
38cm (15in) high

POT SIZE
15cm (6in)

FLOWER
5cm (2in) wide

PLANT
30cm (12in) high

POT SIZE
12cm (5in)

Dendrobium Thongchai Gold

Further distinct breeding lines using Australian and New Guinea species have made a huge variety of colours and flower shapes available. Many new hybrids are raised in Thailand, where the climate ideally suits these warm-growing plants. The species behind Thongchai Gold includes *D. bigibbum*, once known as *D. phalaenopsis*, a highly variable species first described in 1852, having been cultivated at the Royal Botanic Gardens, Kew, since 1824. Thongchai Gold is one of a number which produce yellow-gold flowers, the dark red-mauve lip making a stunning contrast. The petals, narrow at the base, are rounded out at their tips; the smaller sepals may be lighter in colour. The flowers are carried on spikes produced from the top half of the canes.

Dendrobium Siam Jewel

This is a warm-growing, hard-caned *Dendrobium* which, when given sufficient light, will produce sprays of pretty flowers from the top of the elongated pseudobulb throughout the spring. The blooms will last for a good four weeks. Various colours from white and pale pink, through mauve to dark purple have all been derived from species native to Australia. This exceptional hybrid from 1992 borders on the elusive blue. Extremely popular, it is grown worldwide for the pot-plant and cut-flower trade. However, an amateur can re-flower these orchids with the right conditions in a greenhouse: provide good light all year round and maximum temperatures in the warm range where possible. Keep the plants moist while they are growing but allow them to dry out in winter.

FLOWER
7cm (2 ¾in) wide

FLOWER SPIKE
25cm (10in) long

PLANT
30cm (12in) high

POT SIZE
10cm (4in)

Dendrobium **Ruby Beauty**

This is a superb example of a hard-caned *Dendrobium* hybrid, of a type that is widely grown all over the world. Raised in 1990, these orchids are extremely tolerant and adaptable to various climates, but bear in mind that they are tropical plants and in their native environment they make ideal garden plants. A mature plant will produce two to three flower spikes, each with about six or eight flowers, during the autumn from the top portion of the elongated pseudobulbs. The pseudobulbs are leafed all along their length and the leaves are retained during the winter, unlike in many dendrobiums which are deciduous. These hybrids are grown in Singapore and Thailand for the cut-flower trade and are exported far and wide. In florists and elsewhere they are known simply as Singapore orchids, and can be found in a multitude of colours in shops just about anywhere in the world.

Dendrobium All Seasons Blue

All Seasons Blue is one of many hybrids raised from the Australian species of hard-caned dendrobiums. Their more rigid canes remain upright without staking, their flowers produced on spikes from a terminal node in autumn. The equally-proportioned sepals and petals are spread wide, while the lip is small and neat, of similar plain colouring. The parents of this beautiful hybrid, raised in Thailand in 1995, are Pinky Sem and Minnie.

GROWERS' TIP
Grow from 10°C (50°F) min. to 30°C (85°F) max. for best results.

FLOWER
4cm (1½in) wide

FLOWER SPIKE
15cm (6in) long

PLANT
30cm (12in) high

POT SIZE
15cm (6in)

Dendrobium rhodostictum x *atroviolaceum*

This is an unusual hybrid raised from distinctive New Guinea species. The small-growing plant produces club-shaped pseudobulbs with leathery terminal leaves and is compact enough for indoor culture. The extraordinary blooms, whitish with light spotting on the outside of the petals, sport a small, neat, light green lip. Up to six flowers, carried on a loose flower spike, will last for six months or more. The species *D. atroviolaceum* was seen for the first time in 1890 when exhibited at the Royal Horticultural Show in London, the year of its introduction. This species, dominant in the cross shown here, and its hybrids are admired for their fragrant blooms, which are among the longest-lived of all cultivated orchids.

FLOWER
3cm (1¼in) wide

FLOWER SPIKE
10cm (4in) long

PLANT
30cm (12in) high

POT SIZE
10cm (4in)

Dendrobium Dale Takiguchi

This attractive *Phalaenopsis*-type hybrid illustrates the beauty of the
clear, pale coloured flowers which can be produced by breeding
from the white, or albino, forms of the species. This is one of the
hard-caned dendrobiums whose tall canes, pointed at the top, can
remain evergreen for two to three years. The oval leaves cover the
top half of the canes only, unlike the *D.nobile*-type hybrids which
are leafed through their whole length. This plant blooms freely in
the spring and summer months, producing
its lovely flowers on arching sprays, which
will last for several weeks in perfection.
Unlike other dendrobiums, these hybrids
do not grow excessively tall, which makes
them good subjects for a position on a
light windowsill.

FLOWER
6cm (2¹/₂in) wide

FLOWER SPIKE
15cm (6in) long

PLANT
40cm (16in) high

POT SIZE
15cm (6in)

Paphiopedilum Deperle

This is an extremely popular primary hybrid between the Vietnam species *Paphiopedilum delenatii* and the recently discovered Sumatran species, *Paphiopedilum primulinum*. The latter species, described only in 1973, has opened up a new breeding line for small yellow-flowered hybrids and has proved the dominant parent in this 1980 French-bred plant. The compact blooms of Deperle open one at a time; they resemble those of *P. primulinum* in overall shape and their colouring – a delightful soft, buttery yellow – belies the other parent, which usually passes its pink pigment on to its progeny.

FLOWER
6cm (2¹/₂in) wide

FLOWER SPIKE
25cm (10in) long

PLANT
15cm (6in) high

POT SIZE
10cm (4in)

Paphiopedilum villosum

This cool-growing Himalayan species was discovered in 1853, growing epiphytically in the wet, mountainous areas of Burma at an altitude of 2,000m (6,000ft), where the nights are cool. In 1869 it was crossed with *Paphiopedilum barbatum*, a terrestrial Malaysian species with mottled foliage which grows at a lower altitude, to produce *P.* Harrisianum, the first hybrid in the genus. *P. villosum* has slender, dark green foliage and carries a single flower on the stem in late autumn and winter; the colour of polished brass, it has a high gloss to its waxy petals and pouch. This species has been used extensively in the past to produce many of today's fine hybrids, which still retain the shining colours and decoration on the dorsal sepal, but it is now less widely grown as the stock of cultivated plants dwindle and it is no longer available from the wild. The temperature range of this species is lower than that of most other Paphiopedilums, from 10°C (50°F) minimum to 24°C (75°F) maximum.

GROWERS' TIP
This orchid benefits from being kept in a cool and shady place.

FLOWER
10cm (4in) wide

FLOWER SPIKE
15cm (6in) long

PLANT
25cm (10in) high

POT SIZE
10cm (4in)

Paphiopedilum Pinocchio

FLOWER
8cm (3in) wide

FLOWER SPIKE
25cm (10in) long

PLANT
15cm (6in) high

POT SIZE
10cm (4in)

Raised in France in 1977, this is a primary hybrid from two closely related species, *P. primulinum* and *P. glaucophyllum*. With its pretty, compact blooms it is probably the smallest variety in the genus. The centre of the bloom shows a deep green rostellum (similar to the column in other genera) and on either side of the staminode are the pollinia, hidden from view, but against which the pollinating insect must push to find its way out of the pouch. While these orchids do not eat or digest insects, they do trap them when they slip and fall into the pouch. The insect can easily escape, but in doing so either removes or deposits pollen.

Paphiopedilum Jersey Freckles

This handsome Complex hybrid is typical of a multitude of similar hybrids raised from Indian species such as *P. insigne*, *P. villosum* and *P. barbatum*. Breeding continued over many generations to give rise to distinct colours and markings in the form of spots and dashes over a lighter base (see page 46 for a close-up detail of the lip). These hybrids have both cool- and warmer-growing parents in their background. Jersey Freckles is a green-leafed type which may be grown in a warm and shady position indoors or in a heated greenhouse. These plants dislike too much direct light and prefer shadier places where the sun does not reach. A single flower, which can last for up to eight weeks, blooms during the winter months; a large plant will produce more than one flower on separate stems from each new growth.

FLOWER	*12cm (5in) wide*
FLOWER SPIKE	*20cm (8in) long*
PLANT	*12cm (5in) high*
POT SIZE	*10cm (4in)*

Paphiopedilum Chiquita

This is another example of the new breed of paphiopedilums, using *P. primulinum* to bring in a different colour range. This lime-yellow species, found in 1972 in Sumatra at the low altitude of 400m (1,300ft), was one of the best discoveries of that decade. It belongs to a small group of related species with narrow, wavy-edged petals and a distinctive pouch, traits which continue to characterize its hybrids. Here, light orange and peach shades are seen with the pale green dorsal sepal in a pleasing combination. The light, open flower shape is a contrast to the heavy, rounded blooms usually seen within the genus. Several flowers are produced at the end of the spike but only one flower opens at a time.

FLOWER	*8cm (3in) wide*
FLOWER SPIKE	*15cm (6in) long*
PLANT	*13cm (5in) high*
POT SIZE	*10cm (4in)*

Paphiopedilum Gina Short

Pink-flowered paphiopedilums have always been more unusual but are much admired and sought after. Pink colouring was unknown in the genus until the accidental discovery of *P. delenatii* in 1913 by a French soldier fighting in Indochina (now Vietnam). The large flowers usually retain their distinctive shape, with an egg-shaped pouch typical of the species; one to three summer-blooming flowers can be produced on a single short spike. These compact plants also produce exquisite foliage, darkly tessellated on the surface with purple peppering on the undersides of the leaves. Keep the foliage dry because of the danger of water lodging in the centre, which will rot the growth.

FLOWER
10cm (4in) wide

FLOWER SPIKE
12cm (5in) long

PLANT
12cm (5in) high

POT SIZE
10cm (4in)

Paphiopedilum Holdenii

There are a number of these clean, clear, green-flowered types among the mottle-leafed paphiopedilums and all are popular. The dorsal sepal carries the typical 'humbug' stripes while the remainder of the flower is self-coloured. This is an older hybrid, raised in Britain in 1909 from the green-flowered *P. callosum var. sanderae* and *P.* Maudiae, itself a *P. callosum* hybrid. It is still in demand today, along with others which have been bred from it. The attractive light green mottled foliage is compact, with oval leaves. A single bloom, produced on a tall stem, needs the support of a thin bamboo cane to hold the flower upright. Wait until the flower has opened and become set for a few days before tying it back to the cane so that it can be seen facing towards the front.

FLOWER
10cm (4in) wide

FLOWER SPIKE
25cm (10in) long

PLANT
12cm (5in) high

POT SIZE
10cm (4in)

Paphiopedilum Silverlight

Bred along similar lines to *P.* Chiquita (see page 143), this flower exhibits the buttery yellow colouring of *P. primulinum*, the original species from which it was raised. This group of sequential-flowering hybrids prefer a warmer environment, reflecting the original home of the dominant parent species, a low-altitude plant from Sumatra.

Their slender foliage is mid- to light green, indicating their preference for shady conditions. Apart from yellow, light greens and whites are seen in this new line of breeding, gaining popularity with those who prefer smaller flowers.

FLOWER
10cm (4in) wide

FLOWER SPIKE
12cm (5in) long

PLANT
12cm (5in) high

POT SIZE
10cm (4in)

Paphiopedilum spicerianum

Today this Himalayan species is rare, both in the wild and in cultivation, and is found only in specialist collections, but there are a multitude of hybrids available from it. Since its introduction in 1878, when it was named in honour of the grower Herbert Spicer of Surrey, England, it has been used extensively for breeding. The species has oblong green leaves and produces flower spikes with a single green-copper bloom that will last for up to three months during the autumn and winter. The dorsal petal is hooded, which in the wild prevents water from entering the pouch. Water droplets look attractive, as in the photograph on the left, but they can cause damp spots or even bud drop, therefore when misting, take care only to spray the leaves. It can be grown on to produce a large specimen with multiple flowers.

GROWERS' TIP
Water all year round and keep on a cool windowsill for best results.

FLOWER
8cm (3in) wide

FLOWER SPIKE
18cm (7in) long

PLANT
25cm (10in) high

POT SIZE
15cm (6in)

Paphiopedilum Prime Child

This unusual-looking hybrid has been raised from the Borneo species *P. rothschildianum*, noted for its extraordinary long and narrow petals. The downward-swooping petals of Prime Child are spotted along their length. While the species produces multi-flowering spikes, this hybrid flowers in succession like its other parent, *P. primulinum*, with one bud opening at a time. The hybrid was originally raised in California in 1985, since when other nurseries have remade the cross, making it more widely available. Various clones show subtle differences in flower shape.

FLOWER
18cm (7in) wide

FLOWER SPIKE
30cm (12in) long

PLANT
20cm (8in) high

POT SIZE
12cm (5in)

Paphiopedilum Leeanum

This plant is an orchid classic – a very old primary hybrid raised in Britain in 1884, when the first hybrids were appearing among the orchids. From the start, these handsome slipper orchids were in the forefront of this new hybridizing and were among the most popular with the (mostly gentlemen) growers of that time. The parents of this lovely hybrid are *P. insigne* and *P. spicerianum*, two of the most popular orchids of their time, and even today they are both considered to be collectables. Once extremely plentiful, they are now rare in collections, as is the hybrid from them. This plant exhibits all the grace and classic lines of the species. It should be grown in cool, shady conditions and will bloom during the winter. Its single blooms will last eight weeks or more.

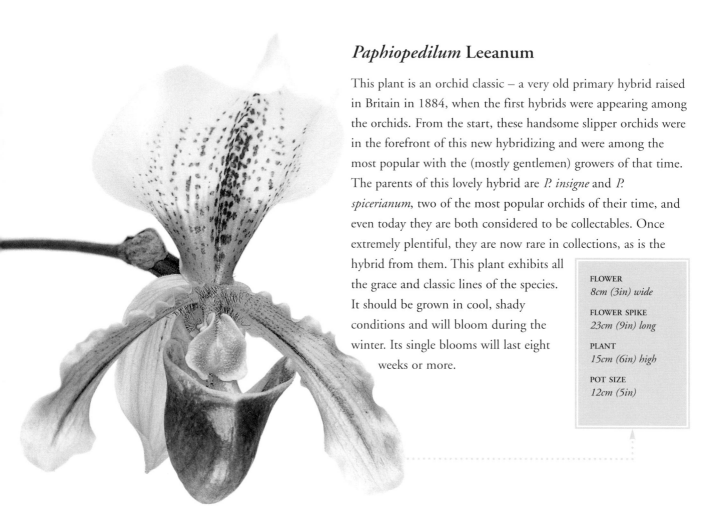

FLOWER
8cm (3in) wide

FLOWER SPIKE
23cm (9in) long

PLANT
15cm (6in) high

POT SIZE
12cm (5in)

Paphiopedilum Jac Flash

This is one of the modern breed of very dark-coloured hybrids produced by crossing with selections of the species *P. callosum*. This terrestrial species is still grown today, with attractive light and dark green mottled foliage and its purple and green flower on a tall, slender stem. Discovered in 1885, it originates from Thailand and Indochina (now Vietnam), and has produced its own brand of desirable hybrids for over 100 years. This hybridization has led to some exciting shades very near to the elusive black. The large, flared dorsal sepal is heavily stained purple, with darker veining, while the swept-down petals are green and purple, and the pouch shows the darkest colour of all. The compact plants also produce attractive mottled foliage, with short, rounded leaves, and make good house-plants even when not in bloom. Jac Flash blooms mainly in summer and will last for several weeks.

FLOWER
5cm (2in) wide

FLOWER SPIKE
25cm (10in) long

PLANT
10cm (4in) high

POT SIZE
12cm (5in)

Phragmipedium longifolium

The dramatic flowers of this wonderful display orchid, with their long, narrow drooping petals, illustrate why phragmipediums are called 'mandarin orchids'. This species is found from Costa Rica to Colombia, where it grows in the leaf litter as a terrestrial. On close inspection, the greenish flowers reveal minute spotting and light striping through the petals and pouch. The green staminode at the centre of the bloom is distinguished by its short fringe of black hairs. It has tall, lush foliage and the extremely long spikes produce many flowers in succession.

FLOWER
12cm (5in) long

FLOWER SPIKE
2m (6ft) long

PLANT
60cm (24in) high

POT SIZE
20cm (8in)

Phragmipedium Sedenii

This beautiful early primary hybrid, 30cm (12in) high, was raised in 1873 by Veitch & Sons. It has stood the test of time and is still available today, though only as a rare collectors' item. The parents are *P. longifolium* and *P. schlimii* and it was produced when raising orchids from seed was hazardous, so only a few plants survived to flowering. The flowers more closely resemble *P. schlimii*, from where it has inherited the light pastel colouring typical of older hybrids and in direct contrast to the bright colours of modern phragmipediums. The tall flower spike carries several buds, not all of which will open at once.

FLOWER
6cm (2¹/₂in) wide

FLOWER SPIKE
45cm (18in) long

PLANT
30cm (12in) high

POT SIZE
12cm (5in)

Phragmipedium besseae

Until this species was discovered in the 1980s, red colouring was unknown in the genus. It has single-handedly been responsible for opening up a new line of highly desirable plants which are free flowering and easy to grow. Its discovery so late was due in part to the plant's habit of growing on inaccessible rock faces in its native home high in the Andes in Ecuador and Peru. Much sought after by collectors today, the species has given rise to numerous vibrant red and orange hybrids, the like of which was unthinkable a few years ago. The plant produces tufted growths along a creeping rhizome and blooms mainly in autumn, producing its small flowers in

succession on a long spike. The oval petals and sides of the pouch have clear, almost transparent sections, but the flower's most notable feature is its brilliant pelargonium-red colour.

FLOWER
8cm (3in) wide

FLOWER SPIKE
30cm (12in) long

PLANT
25cm (10in) high

POT SIZE
15cm (6in)

Phragmipedium Grouville

Similar breeding lines can reveal surprises in the range of colours produced, as with this light pink variation among red-flowered hybrids. Grouville's flowers exhibit the familiar classic shape but with pastel rather than rich red hues. A generation on from Eric Young (see page 157), the flower shape reflects the continuing influence of *P. besseae*, which more usually imparts the red colouring to its hybrids. With further buds extending the flower spike, the plant will remain in flower for months before the last flower drops. These lovely, bright hybrids still hold novelty value for the collector and amateur grower but there is no doubt they have a great future ahead.

FLOWER
8cm (3in) wide

FLOWER SPIKE
30cm (12in) long

PLANT
20cm (8in) high

POT SIZE
12cm (5in)

Phragmipedium Beauport

This hybrid was raised in 1997 at the Eric Young Orchid Foundation in the Channel Islands, using the light green-flowered Brazilian species *P. sargentianum*, introduced in 1892, and the red-flowered hybrid from *P. besseae*, Hanne Popow. Rounded petals and an egg-shaped pouch set the hybrid apart, combined with its deep, rosy red colouring. The small dorsal sepal is similarly coloured, and the flowers are produced in succession on an extending upright flower spike which may not require tying. The plant blooms in late spring from the previous season's growth. While these orchids will divide when there are enough growths to one plant, if left to reach specimen size they will produce multiple flower spikes at a time, giving a really impressive show of blooms.

Phragmipedium St Ouen

Another extremely desirable hybrid raised along similar lines, this gives further variety of shape and colour. The deep pink has come from the parent *P. besseae*, which also shows in the rigidly held, broad pointed petals. The pouch is prettily striped with a prominent yellow staminode at the centre. The other parent is Hanne Popow, a *P. besseae* hybrid, representing the main line from which we expect the finest hybrids in this range. As each flower ages, it drops from the stem while another takes its place, as can be seen on the lower stem, in the illustration above. In this way the plant will remain in bloom for months on end, making this genus probably the longest-lived in its flowering season.

FLOWER
8cm (3in) wide

FLOWER SPIKE
30cm (12in) long

PLANT
20cm (8in) high

POT SIZE
12cm (5in)

Phragmipedium Don Wimber

In this exciting, richly coloured modern hybrid the flower is distinctly triangular in shape, complemented by a well-balanced pouch. It was raised in Jersey in 1995 from parent plant Eric Young (see page 157), crossed back onto *P. besseae* to retain the best of the colouring which distinguishes this group. The flowers appear on a tall spike, which produces further buds from the apex as it extends. The plant is a strong, robust grower with long, strap-like leaves of mid-green. These orchids like to be kept well watered throughout the year so their fleshy leaves do not become dehydrated or limp. Light spraying is beneficial, provided water does not lodge inside the growths.

FLOWER
10cm (4in) wide

FLOWER SPIKE
60cm (24in) long

PLANT
45cm (18in) high

POT SIZE
20cm (8in)

Phragmipedium St Peter

The 'Saints' series all come from the Eric Young Orchid Foundation in the Channel Islands, whose fame has spread worldwide. St Peter is a further variation on the theme of red-flowered hybrids; its parents are Eric Young (see page 157), a primary cross between species *P. longifolium* and *P. besseae* raised in 1991, and the species *P. longifolium* (see page 150) itself, which therefore occurs twice in two generations of this delightful hybrid. The flower spikes are tall and gracious and need plenty of headroom if they are to be grown well. This long-petalled hybrid carries a more open pouch, which is a distinctive feature of the flower.

FLOWER
12cm (5in) wide

FLOWER SPIKE
45cm (18in) long

PLANT
30cm (12in) high

POT SIZE
15cm (6in)

Phragmipedium Corbière

Among the latest *Phragmipedium* hybrids are
those produced from the long-petalled species.
Their main feature shows up well in this
desirable hybrid, crossing the well-tested
flame-coloured Eric Young with an older, long-
petalled primary hybrid, Calurum. Several
long-lasting, light red blooms are produced on
a tall flower spike. The close-up clearly shows
the intriguing formation of the pouch, or
slipper. The leaves are long and strap-like and
the plant needs plenty of space to grow well.
Since its introduction in 1996, this modern
flower has gained worldwide popularity.

FLOWER
10cm (4in) wide

FLOWER SPIKE
60cm (24in) long

PLANT
45cm (18in) high

POT SIZE
20cm (8in)

Phragmipedium Eric Young

This distinctively shaped flower positively glows with warm orange
tones, while its long, semi-drooping petals sweep down from the
horizontal, half-encircling the pouch. To date this is one of the
finest of the new hybrids achieved through the introduction of the
magnificent *P. besseae*, which readily imparts its unique red
colouring to its progeny; the other parent is
P. longifolium. The hybrid was raised in
1991, since when it has gone on to produce
further generations. The large flowers are
not heavily textured and are easily
supported on the upright flower spike; the
small dorsal sepal is another feature of this
line of breeding.

FLOWER
10cm (4in) wide

FLOWER SPIKE
60cm (24in) long

PLANT
45cm (18in) high

POT SIZE
20cm (8in)

Epidendrum pseudepidendrum

The epidendrums are a genus of many tall-growing plants with thin, leafy canes, or with slender, one-leafed pseudobulbs which resemble cattleyas. Species from the latter group have been crossed with cattleyas to produce the bigeneric hybrid genus of Epicattleya, among others. *E. pseudepidendrum* belongs to the reed-type epidendrums, as the other group is known, which contain some extremely interesting orchids that exhibit strange formations and colourings. This species comes from Costa Rica where it grows on trees as an epiphyte, producing extensive stems that bloom from the apex when growth is completed. Several flowers are produced on an arching stem, a combination of bright green, narrowly long sepals and petals with a contrasting bright orange lip, which is glossy, waxy and almost plastic in appearance.

GROWERS' TIP
Ensure you leave this tall-growing species with plenty of head room.

FLOWER
5cm (2in) wide

FLOWER SPIKE
15cm (6in) long

PLANT
30–100cm (12–40in) high

POT SIZE
18cm (7in)

Epidendrum Plastic Doll

Looking at the flower shape and coloration of this unusual hybrid, bred in Japan in 1989, it becomes obvious that one parent is the bright *E. pseudepidendrum* (see left). There is a close resemblance both in its flowers, especially the protruding lip, and the plant's overall habit; the other parent is *E. ilense*. Plastic Doll blooms over a long period in summer, after which it rests and needs less water. Leaves are shed a few at a time from the older canes, which eventually become completely leafless before shrivelling and dying. The plants do best in fairly small (15-cm/6-in) pots, but they need a supporting cane.

FLOWER
5cm (2in) wide

FLOWER SPIKE
15cm (6in) long

PLANT
30–100cm (12–40in) high

POT SIZE
15cm (6in)

Epidendrum Pink Cascade

Among the tall-growing, reed-type epidendrums there has been only limited hybridizing, often with disappointing results as little advancement is seen to be made. This hybrid is an exception, however, and has proved to be a delightful addition to their numbers. The parents of this British-bred primary hybrid are *E. ilense* (see page 162) and *E. revolutum*; it was raised in 1990 by Burnham Nurseries in Devon, England. The plants are not so tall as to be difficult to accommodate within the home and they bloom on young stems, leafed throughout their length. Numerous pink flowers with rigid, outstretched petals, are produced on an arching stem which is an extension of the leafy growth; more blooms appear over a period of time, which lengthens the flowering season. The pretty, marked flowers are also individually long-lasting.

FLOWER
5cm (2in) wide

FLOWER SPIKE
15cm (6in) long

PLANT
60cm (24in) high

POT SIZE
15cm (6in)

Epidendrum ciliare

Originating in the West Indies and tropical America, this *Epidendrum* is one of a group of similar species which produce slender pseudobulbs with a solitary leaf, not unlike the growth of many sophronitis, with which they can be interbred. It was described in 1759, making it one of the earliest-known of the tropical epiphytes. The flowers are produced on a lengthy stem from the top of the latest pseudobulb. Up to eight flowers are produced, which have long, narrow, light green petals and sepals, with an equally long, deeply lobed white lip, frilled at the edge. This is another manifestation of the bearding which appears on the lips of various orchids, its precise function is unknown. The autumn-blooming species can be shy to flower if not given sufficient light, particularly towards the end of summer when the pseudobulbs are maturing.

FLOWER
9cm (3¹/₂in) wide

FLOWER SPIKE
15cm (6in) long

PLANT
30cm (12in) high

POT SIZE
15cm (6in)

Epidendrum centradenia

This delightful little species from central South America, whose genus was first described in 1852, is just one example of how some of the smallest orchids can be so appealing and worth growing alongside the larger, more flamboyant types. Plants of this stature take up little room and can be a real boon where space is limited. You could

also try growing this species in a cool, disused fish tank, where you can create a humid environment by placing pebbles in the base and keeping them wet. This is a neat plant with slender, cane-like stems and narrow leaves. The flowers are borne in spring on a spike at the top of the mature cane, with up to six flowers to a spike that will last for about three weeks.

FLOWER
1cm (1/2in) wide

FLOWER SPIKE
10cm (4in) long

PLANT
15cm (6in) high

POT SIZE
6cm (2 1/2in)

GROWERS' TIP
This unusual plant needs a fairly large container to prevent it getting top-heavy.

FLOWER
5cm (2in) wide

FLOWER SPIKE
15cm (6in) long

PLANT
30–100cm (12–40in) high

POT SIZE
18cm (7in)

Epidendrum ilense

This robust, tall-growing species from Central America produces leafy stems that bloom from the apex when growth is complete. A recent introduction, it was discovered during the latter decades of the twentieth century, growing in a small area of Costa Rica. The extraordinary flowers are carried on a slender, arching stem and appear in succession over a long period, with three to four blooms out at any one time. Their colour is off-white, the sepals and petals small but the lip strangely bulbous at the centre, its edge deeply frilled to give a bearded effect. Old, leafless stems continue to produce blooms over several years.

Epidendrum wallisii

This is one of a group of mainly summer-flowering epidendrums which can be grown where there is sufficient headroom for their tall, leafy stems to extend unhindered. At the apex are these delightful flowers, regally coloured with purple-spotted yellow petals and sepals, swept back to emphasize the deeply lobed, blue-violet lip. This terrestrial species was discovered in Colombia in 1875 by the orchid collector, Gustav Wallis, growing at an elevation of 1,500m (5,000ft). While these are vigorous growers, they do not divide or propagate easily and you must be prepared for the plants to become very large over a period of several years. Only when they have reached specimen size, with several new growths all blooming at the same time, can they be viewed at their full potential.

FLOWER
5cm (2in) wide

FLOWER SPIKE
15cm (6in) long

PLANT
45cm (18in) high

POT SIZE
12cm (5in)

Coelogyne speciosa

A number of tall-growing *Coelogyne* species are remarkable for their amazing lip markings and coloration. This species from Sumatra exhibits the best qualities of the group: the flowers are large, the sepals light buff or cream, with the slender, hardly visible petals hidden behind the sepals. The lip, covered with ridges and fine hairs, is a deep chocolate brown at the centre. The plant produces cone-shaped pseudobulbs with two widely oval leaves; the flower spikes come from the centre of the new growth while it is at a young stage. Several blooms are produced, but only one opens at a

time, spreading the flowering season over several weeks in late summer. The modest amount of hybridizing that has been done with this species shows little improvement over the species itself.

FLOWER
6cm (2¹/2in) wide

PLANT
30cm (12in) high

POT SIZE
15cm (6in)

Coelogyne Green Dragon 'Chelsea' AM/RHS

Among the most easily grown coelogynes are a number from Malaysia which need warmer conditions. They are larger in their growth and produce correspondingly bigger flowers, but where there is enough room for their lush foliage, they offer dramatic colour and flowering habits. This unusual clone retains the apple-green colouring of one parent species, *C. pandurata*, with the intricate lip markings of the other, *C. tomentosa* (see right). The flowers are produced theatrically – the spike pushes up and out of the new growth to plunge vertically in an extending chain until the buds swell and open their flowers.

FLOWER
10cm (4in) wide

FLOWER SPIKE
30cm (12in) long

PLANT
45cm (18in) high

POT SIZE
20cm (8in)

Coelogyne tomentosa

This tall-growing species makes an impressive
plant with large, oval pseudobulbs topped by two
wide, oval leaves. The flower spikes emerge from the young
new growth and plunge dramatically over the side of the pot
to bloom vertically along its length. Numerous flowers, light
buff-brown with yellow and brown markings on the lip, are
produced in the spring and last for up to three weeks. The species
comes from Malaysia and Borneo where it grows on trees in
mountainous regions. It has been in cultivation
for many years and propagates freely,
maintaining a steady plant population.

FLOWER
4cm (1¹/₂in) wide

FLOWER SPIKE
30cm (12in) long

PLANT
60cm (24in) high

POT SIZE
25cm (10in)

Ludisia discolor

This attractive terrestrial species from China and South-East Asia is grown as much for its foliage as its flowers. It is one of a number known as 'jewel orchids', because of the delicate veining which shows red on the dark, velvety green leaves. In their natural habitat these plants grow in deep shade and humid conditions in mossy banks along rivers. The plant forms leafy growths along a creeping rhizome; when growth is completed, a flowering stem arises from the centre; its intricate white blooms resembling little bees flying. Keep this evergreen species moist all year, but without too much humidity around it. It needs a minimum winter temperature of 13°C (55°F).

Barkeria lindleyana

There are many delightful miniature orchids that will grace any collection, taking up very little space on a windowsill. This species from Guatemala, discovered in 1842, is one of them. In its native habitat it can be found growing on trees or rocks, where it will develop into quite a large plant. In cultivation, however, it remains compact, producing its small stem-like growths and up to six deep cerise, yellow-centered flowers on a slender flower spike above the foliage. The blooms will last for two to three weeks in autumn.

Aspasia lunata

This is a small-growing, lesser-known member of the *Odontoglossum* alliance, grown for its attraction as a species in its own right. It produces small, lengthened pseudobulbs with a pair of narrow leaves and will quickly establish itself as a specimen if left undivided for a few years. In addition to being grown in a pot, this species can also grow in a hanging basket. Its early summer flowers are carried on shortened spikes, with a single star-shaped bloom. The narrow petals and sepals are green, speckled with brown, and the flared lip is white, with rosy mauve towards the centre. The flowers most closely resemble brassias and will cross-breed with them and related orchids.

FLOWER
5cm (2in) wide

PLANT
15cm (6in) high

POT SIZE
12cm (5in)

Zygopetalum maxillare

This is a plant for the collector. The species comes from Brazil where it grows epiphytically, producing its scant pseudobulbs wide apart along a strong, creeping and upright rhizome. It has several long, narrow mid-green leaves, as well as short aerial roots at regular intervals along the stem. The plant is best grown in a pot into which a mossy pole has been inserted, or it may be grown on a stout piece of cork bark with a pad of sphagnum moss tied to it, into which the roots will grow and gather moisture. Waxy, fragrant flowers, up to six or eight on a spike, appear in autumn. They are among the most colourful orchids in the genus, which is remarkable for the sombre purple and brown colouring characteristic of most other species. The close-up shown here reveals the dark purple colouring which radiates out across the lip, while the light green petals and sepals are heavily overlaid with bronzy-brown.

GROWERS' TIP
Do not spray the foliage on this plant as it may cause spotting on the leaves.

FLOWER
5cm (2in) wide

FLOWER SPIKE
30cm (12in) long

PLANT
90cm (36in) high

POT SIZE
15cm (6in)

Zygopetalum Luisendorf

Zygopetalums are becoming more and more popular as new varieties
and hybrids that are easy to grow and bloom freely come onto the
market. Bred from species originally imported from Brazil, the
dominant colours have always been green and brown. By incorporating
other species, new colours are being created to greatly extend the range
and desirability. This new hybrid produces a compact plant which
blooms from the latest pseudobulb throughout autumn. The fragrant
blooms, two to three at a time, are held at the end of the flower spike
and will last for three to four weeks. They are light olive-brown with a
large, spreading purple lip that is deeply veined and coloured. Grow in
cool to intermediate temperatures in a well-drained compost to prevent
the plant from getting too wet in winter.

FLOWER
6cm (2¹/2in) wide

FLOWER SPIKE
30cm (12in) long

PLANT
25cm (10in) high

POT SIZE
12cm (5in)

Warm-growing orchids

Those orchids included in the warm-growing range require temperatures that are higher at night but not necessarily by day. Since they do not need the same variation as cooler-growing orchids, this makes them ideal garden plants in tropical parts of the world, where temperatures fluctuate by only a few degrees between day and night, summer and winter. The same orchids also grow well indoors in more temperate climates, where overnight central heating provides minimum background warmth of 18°C (64°F). The year-round daytime temperature can be the same as for cooler-growing orchids in summer, or a little higher. As the temperature range decreases, so does the variety of plants that can be accommodated in the narrower band.

Phalaenopsis Golden Bells

This very pretty variety has distinct deep yellow dotting over a pale yellow ground, which gives a pleasing, unusual combination. The russet-red highlight at the centre of the white lip gives the whole flower a bright appearance. Golden Bells has the well-known yellow Golden Sands as one parent, while the other, the species *P. venosa*, has shortened the flowering spikes. The yellow hybrids produce slightly smaller flowers which keep their colour throughout the long flowering period, and the more compact flower spike will remain upright without the need for a supporting cane, making this an ideal plant to grow where space is limited.

FLOWER
6cm (2¹/₂in) wide

FLOWER SPIKE
25cm (10in) long

PLANT
20cm (8in) high

POT SIZE
10cm (4in)

Phalaenopsis Paifang's Golden Lion

Heavy leopard spotting overlies this lighter-based flower, giving the impression of deep rosy-purple. The lateral petals are neatly divided along the centre vein, below which the colour becomes intensified. Such exquisite colouring is found only in this type of hybrid which produces glossy, waxy-textured flowers in a perfectly symmetrical shape on a shorter stem; the individual flowers, produced in succession, remain a long time in bloom. As mature flowers fade, new buds are continually opening along an extending stem. Paifang's Golden Queen is the mother plant of the selective breeding line that has produced many superb spotted hybrids from a pink form of the variable species, *P. lueddemanniana*. This particular hybrid was raised in 1992 by Paifang's Orchid Garden in Taiwan.

FLOWER
8cm (3in) wide

FLOWER SPIKE
23cm (9in) long

PLANT
20cm (8in) high

POT SIZE
10cm (4in)

Phalaenopsis Follett

In this luscious hybrid the petal decoration of delicate veining and stripes has been taken to its full potential and the perfectly shaped flowers are enhanced by the deeper lip. This Californian-bred hybrid, raised in 1993, is the result of a long line of specialized breeding from Doris, an important breeding plant of its day, raised in 1940. The hybrid has come so far that it now bears little resemblance to the original tall-flowered Philippines species. The popular, beautifully decorative orchids are often sold under the name 'candy stripes'. Well-grown, mature plants of candy-striped hybrids produce long, branching flower spikes whose blooms open from the lowest on a stem to the buds at the end in less than a week.

FLOWER
8cm (3in) wide

FLOWER SPIKE
75cm (30in) long

PLANT
30cm (12in) high

POT SIZE
12cm (5in)

Phalaenopsis Hawaiian Darling

This delightful modern hybrid was raised in Hawaii, where many new variants are emerging. It is the result of back-crossing the large, pink-flowered hybrid Lippegruss, of German origin, with the delicate, showy *P. stuartiana*, from the Philippines. This species carries many flowers on a tall spike, the blooms white with brown leopard spotting on the lateral sepals and lip. In this new hybrid, the marking has come through as rosy-mauve spotting on the lower sepals, which are partially hidden by the well-rounded petals. The basically white flower has a slight pink flush retained from the pink hybrid parent. Another desirable quality is the arching habit of the spike, which naturally arranges the blooms in a descending spray. The plant will bloom two to three times a year, the long-lasting flowers remaining for several weeks.

FLOWER
6cm (2¹/₂in) wide

FLOWER SPIKE
75cm (30in) long

PLANT
10cm (4in) high

POT SIZE
10cm (4in)

Phalaenopsis San Luca

FLOWER
9cm (3¹/₂in) wide

FLOWER SPIKE
75cm (30in) long

PLANT
30cm (12in) high

POT SIZE
12cm (5in)

The rich red colouring of this fine, modern hybrid is uncommon and has been achieved only by the dedication of the hybridizers, in this instance in California, where young plants can be brought to flowering size in the shortest possible time. Similar breeding through successive generations, as in Follett, has produced a combination of the splash-petal effect behind the candy-striped veining, offset by the ruby-red lip. The large blooms are produced on the end of tall flower spikes with several nodes along their length. When the initial flowering has finished, further branches of flowers can be activated by cutting the end of the stem back to a lower node; while this can be done with almost any *Phalaenopsis*, it is most successful with the long-stemmed kinds. Secondary flowerings produce smaller flowers, however, and they must not be encouraged at the expense of a plant that is to be grown on for a number of years, since excessive flowering will only weaken it.

Phalaenopsis Brother Buddha

The Brother hybrids are the result of a huge wave of hybridizing in Taiwan, this one a cross between Fortune Buddha and Brother Angel, raised in 1992 by Brothers Orchid Nursery. The yellow-flowered hybrids generally produce slightly smaller flowers but their reduced size is more than made up for by the lovely colouring and patterning which overlays many of this type. The plants are more compact and the flower spikes shorter with, usually, less flowers on a spike. The

blooms are neatly placed on the stem and displayed horizontally, rather than drooping on long arching or pendant spikes, as seen in the white, pink and newer red varieties. Once the flowers begin to age, they lose a little of their brightness and tone down to a paler shade. Individual blooms often look almost transparent before falling from the stem.

FLOWER
6cm (2¹/2in) wide

FLOWER SPIKE
25cm (10in) long

PLANT
30cm (12in) high

POT SIZE
12cm (5in)

FLOWER
9cm (3½in) wide

FLOWER SPIKE
75cm (30in) long

PLANT
30cm (12in) high

POT SIZE
12cm (5in)

Phalaenopsis Culiacan

A flower with pearl-white sepals and petals and a clean yellow lip makes a beautiful contrast. This flower's appearance is perhaps close to the original species which so captivated the early explorers when they hunted these exotic blooms in the topmost branches of giant trees in the Philippine Islands. This French-bred hybrid is the latest in a long line of thoroughbreds which have been kept pure of colour. Its parents are Gatto and Fairy Tales, raised in 1992 by Zuma Canyon of California. The breeding goes back many generations to Cassandra, a stepping-stone parent and primary hybrid raised by Veitch in 1896 from *P. equestris* and *P. stuartiana*.

Phalaenopsis Sweet Memory

A further dimension has been created by the introduction of breeding from the species, *P. violacea*, which has here been crossed with an older primary hybrid, Deventeriana (1927). While *P. violacea* has dominated the texture, shape and lip of Sweet Memory, the rich colouring comes from Deventeriana. The individual flowers are richly coloured, with darker overtones on a light base, which contrasts with the deep red of the lip. The blooms have a heavier texture and a more open shape than more conventional hybrids. These plants can become considerably large-leafed, producing tall, branching flower spikes to give a wonderful show; summer appears to be their peak flowering period. The original cross has been remade for modern breeding purposes, Sweet Memory being typical of the exciting hybrids within this group.

FLOWER
8cm (3in) wide

FLOWER SPIKE
60cm (24in) long

PLANT
38cm (15in) high

POT SIZE
15cm (6in)

Phalaenopsis Pink Twilight

This appealing flower is typical of the pink-flowered hybrids raised using successive generations of pink Philippines species such as, in this case, *P. schilleriana* and *P. sanderiana*. Pink Twilight has large, showy blooms, with the flowers arranged neatly along two sides of the stem. The stem assumes an arching habit under its own weight as the flowers open: these blooms can be produced at various times of the year and last for many weeks. The intricate detail of the lip is shown enlarged to reveal the minute decoration and rather mysterious shape, which spell out a direct message to the pollinating insect. Hybridizing has greatly enhanced the lip decoration to match our idea of what is attractive. Many different varieties can be found in this colour range, all of which will produce flowers two or three times a year.

FLOWER
8cm (3in) wide

FLOWER SPIKE
30cm (12in) long

PLANT
30cm (12in) high

POT SIZE
12cm (5in)

Phalaenopsis Romantic Tango

Having produced numerous hybrids among the clear white and pretty pink types, the challenge for breeders was to move on to a semi-alba flower with white or pale pink petals and sepals and to combine the pastel colouring with a rich, darker-coloured lip. This modern French-bred hybrid is the latest in a long line of such colour variants: its parents are Culiba and Boutique, a Dutch hybrid raised in 1994. The influence of natural hybrid *P. x intermedia* gives the large, ruby-red lip. The flowers are produced on long sprays; their petals overlap each other. These hybrids will bloom at any time, on tall spikes, and their colouring can vary according to the season. The colour of flowers produced in spring and summer, when the light is brighter, will be more intense than those produced in winter.

FLOWER
8cm (3in) wide

FLOWER SPIKE
45cm (18in) long

PLANT
30cm (12in) high

POT SIZE
12cm (5in)

Phalaenopsis Fajen's Fireworks

Hybrids produced in one part of the world will often run alongside similar developments in other countries, as all breeders of fine orchids are looking for similar attributes. This example shows a line of breeding popular in France, where plants grown under a particular set of climatic conditions are produced for a world market, which means they may finish up growing in any country, often far from that of their raising. Such is the versatility of these vigorous plants that they will grow in any situation where they are kept warm and comfortable, and their few requirements are catered for. Fajen's Fireworks is produced by the Florida nursery, Fajen's Orchids and Exotics, which has used the same line of breeding, starting with the species *P. stuartiana* and *P. x intermedia*, to produce this particular hybrid from Dame de Coeur and Kathleen Ai in 1991. The line veining throughout the petals, breaking up into delicate spotting on the lower sepals, forms the perfect backdrop to the intensified lip colour which is this hybrid's main feature.

FLOWER
8cm (3in) wide

FLOWER SPIKE
45cm (18in) long

PLANT
30cm (12in) high

POT SIZE
12cm (5in)

Phalaenopsis Lipperose

This delicately-coloured, German-bred hybrid is a winner. It was raised in 1968 from Ruby Wells and Zada and represents a long line of quality pink-flowered hybrids which have become popular around the world. In its day it was ahead of its time, producing the first of the large, pink flowers and regarded as a breakthrough in the breeding of quality phalaenopsis, which was previously led by the whites. The soft hues have been retained from the original species. A well-grown plant which misses a flowering can sometimes be encouraged to bloom by lowering the minimum temperature for a few weeks, which will almost certainly initiate the flower spike into activity.

FLOWER
8cm (3in) wide

FLOWER SPIKE
30cm (12in) long

PLANT
30cm (12in) high

POT SIZE
12cm (5in)

Phalaenopsis Yellow Treasure

Yellow Treasure is an example of the lovely, clear yellow hybrids available to those who prefer flowers which are plain and simple. It is one of the latest yellow hybrids to come from the Pacific rim, from where the expanding nurseries are now exporting to a worldwide market. Yellow-flowered phalaenopsis vary from almost white flowers, with pale yellow radiating out from the centre, to the deep, self-coloured hybrids which take on an almost golden tinge. They contrast sharply with lime-coloured flowers, which can look cool on the hottest day.

FLOWER
8cm (3in) wide

FLOWER SPIKE
30cm (12in) long

PLANT
30cm (12in) high

POT SIZE
12cm (5in)

Phalaenopsis Little Skipper

A pretty group known as the Little Guys, these miniature hybrids produce numerous flowers on compact plants and can be relied on to bloom several times during the year. On occasion they may become almost perpetually blooming, with new flower spikes being produced before the last one has lost its blooms. The main colourings within this small group are pink, or pink and white, with deeper red lips in harmony with the rest of the flower. The gracefully arching flower spikes become pendant if unsupported, and their main flowering peaks during autumn and winter. Little Skipper is a 1991 hybrid from California, one of a new line of breeding which may still have much to show us in future generations.

FLOWER
5cm (2in) wide

FLOWER SPIKE
23cm (9in) long

PLANT
15cm (6in) high

POT SIZE
10cm (4in)

Phalaenopsis Petite Snow

Selective breeding from the smaller species within the genus has resulted in a much reduced flower, produced in quantity on a compact flower spike. Petite Snow is an offspring of the much-used breeding parent, Cassandra. Crossed back on to the species *P. stuartiana* in 1985 by Richella in Hawaii, it has itself gone on to produce further notable hybrids of the smaller type. This little gem combines the qualities of the larger types in cheerful rosy pink colourings and is ideal where space is more limited, or when the collection becomes larger as more plants are added. The flowers open all together on the spike, which arches naturally and needs little support. It is not unusual for this type to produce more than one flower spike at a time, giving an excellent show of blooms for its size.

FLOWER
5cm (2in) wide

FLOWER SPIKE
23cm (9in) long

PLANT
15cm (6in) high

POT SIZE
10cm (4in)

Phalaenopsis Hisa Lady Rose

FLOWER
9cm (3¹/₂in) wide

FLOWER SPIKE
75cm (30in) long

PLANT
30cm (12in) high

POT SIZE
12cm (5in)

Hisa Lady Rose, a cross between Otohime and Paradise Glow, was raised in 1988 in Japan and is the latest in a long line of Japanese-bred plants, using the well-known Doris and its offspring Zada as starting points. These parent plants are American- and German-bred hybrids respectively, making the new lines truly global. Phalaenopsis are among the most rewarding orchids for the beginner to grow because of their willingness to grow and flower in conditions which are found in most homes. Treated with care, the plants will live for many years without becoming too large or difficult to handle. Their size is self-regulating as the older leaves are shed to make way for the formation of new ones from the centre of the plant.

Phalaenopsis Pinlong Gleam

This hybrid, raised in 1982 by a Taiwan nursery, is the product of several instances of *P. pulcherrima* arising in its pedigree, with different clones being used. Also in the breeding line appear Doris and Zada, the same hybrids giving a variety of results when used in different combinations. These flowers have a more open, starry appearance with an intensity of colour seldom found in *Phalaenopsis*. Small flowers are produced on an upright flower spike, the petals and sepals slightly concave along their length.

FLOWER
8cm (3in) wide

FLOWER SPIKE
30cm (12in) long

PLANT
30cm (12in) high

POT SIZE
12cm (5in)

Phalaenopsis Quevedo

This extremely pretty hybrid has originated from California and is one of a cluster raised from smaller-flowered species such as *P. equestris*, which has numerous pink flowers on a short spike. This species was crossed with the larger, white-flowered species *P. stuartiana* to produce the primary hybrid, Cassandra, which became a popular breeding plant. Two generations on, and with the input of the white-flowered *P. pulcherrima* var. *alba*, this lovely white-flowered hybrid has appeared. The freely branching spike has come from the *P. equestris* ancestor, whose shape is slightly discernible in the long lip. This hybrid gives a fantastic show of bloom on a compact plant, with its pleasing contrast of white petals and cherry-red lip.

FLOWER
5cm (2in) wide

FLOWER SPIKE
75cm (30in) long

PLANT
10cm (4in) high

POT SIZE
10cm (4in)

Phalaenopsis pulcherrima 'Chumpenensis'

A smaller *Phalaenopsis*, this delightful clone of the species is becoming popular in its own right, as well as for the hybrids raised from it. Originally discovered in 1833 in Vietnam, the pretty *P. pulcherrima* is highly variable and several colour forms are known. Vertical flower spikes are produced whose small, prettily coloured blooms open in succession until the whole spike is in full flower. 'Chumpenensis' is an unusual clone of a species which is normally rose-purple or lilac-purple; these flowers show a rare mutation where the yellow lip markings are repeated on the petals. The blooms, which appear at any time of year, will last for several weeks.

FLOWER
2cm (1in) wide

FLOWER SPIKE
30cm (12in) long

PLANT
15cm (6in) high

POT SIZE
10cm (4in)

Asconopsis Pulcherrimum

By crossing *Phalaenopsis* with *Ascocentrum*, a further breeding line opens up to give highly coloured flowers of a distinct shape and a great deal of character. This hybrid genus was registered in 1969; more recently, a cross between *P. pulcherrima* and *A. miniatum* was raised in Florida but, apart from these, very few other hybrids have appeared in this bigeneric genus. The flat sepals and petals are held rigidly outwards, while the lip has a unique shape, inherited from the *Ascocentrum* parent. These dainty blooms are carried on an upright flower spike, which is self-supporting; summer is the peak flowering season. Since this type of breeding is relatively new, such hybrids are most likely to be found in specialist nurseries, where their bright colours and pleasing flowers ensure they are in great demand.

FLOWER
1cm (¹/2in) wide

FLOWER SPIKE
15cm (6in) long

PLANT
10cm (4in) high

POT SIZE
10cm (4in)

Schlechterara Su-Fun Beauty 'Orange Bell'

Allied to the vandas are several genera which will readily interbreed to produce further man-made intergeneric hybrids, which has greatly extended the variety to be found among this alliance. The genus *Ascocentrum* has a few especially brightly coloured species which, when crossed with vandas, produce some of the most brilliant shades in the orchid family. Such a species is *Ascocentrum miniatum*, whose *Ascocenda* hybrids produce smaller but brighter flowers in fiery orange, red and purple, preferred by many growers. Su-Fun Beauty, raised in Malaysia in 1984, comes from a long line of similar hybrids extending from *Ascocentrum miniatum*, *A. curvifolium* and *Vanda coerulea* as well as *E.sanderianum* on the *Euanthe* side.

FLOWER
9cm (3¹/2in) wide

FLOWER SPIKE
20cm (8in) long

PLANT
45cm (18in) high

POT SIZE
12cm (5in)

Schlechterara Fuchs Yellow Snow

Adding a further colour dimension to the already impressive range of hues found in the genus, this plant offers a speckled white and yellow combination in which the dorsal sepal resembles the petals and the lower sepals are tinged with yellow, overlaid with red-brown tessellating. This new hybrid was raised in Florida in 1991 from *Ascocenda* Phak Hai x *Vanda* Charlie Clark. The *Ascocenda* influence has been largely erased by breeding, leaving a large, *Euanthe sanderiana*-type bloom, whose influence is clearly visible in the patterning on the lower sepals.

FLOWER
6cm (2¹/2in) wide

FLOWER SPIKE
30cm (12in) long

PLANT
45cm (18in) high

POT SIZE
12cm (5in)

Schlechterara Fuchs Flame

This is a further richly coloured hybrid, raised in 1985 by crossing *Vanda* Laksi with the species *Ascocentrum curvifolium*. Since the parents of Laksi are *V.* Thonglor and *A. curvifolium*, a double dose of this latter species has given closely packed blooms of dense, intense colouring on upright flower spikes. The hybrid is extremely free-flowering in good conditions; while mainly summer-blooming, it may also bloom at almost any time of year. An important aspect of the cultivation of ascocendas is the humidity level, which should always balance the high temperatures which are key for the successful culture of these plants.

FLOWER
4cm (1½in) wide

FLOWER SPIKE
20cm (8in) long

PLANT
45cm (18in) high

POT SIZE
12cm (5in)

Schlechterara Fuchs Sunkist 'Mike' AM/AOS

This superb hybrid, raised in Florida in 1987 and awarded by the American Orchid Society, reflects the colours of the tropical sun under which it has been grown. Robert Fuchs is one of today's leading hybridizers in these orchids, his Florida nursery world-renowned. The parents of this hybrid are Yasathon and Laksi and it can be traced back through several generations of schlechterara before reaching any vandas. Best maintained in a warm greenhouse, this hybrid is but a sample of the gorgeous 'jewels of the orient' being produced for the home grower. Raised under shade-cloth houses, and suspended from overhead wires in open slatted baskets, these orchids adopt their natural epiphytic habits and, in response to regular soakings with water, produce long and fleshy aerial roots through which they breathe and absorb moisture. See page 57 for another view of this plant.

FLOWER
9cm (3¹/2in) wide

FLOWER SPIKE
20cm (8in) long

PLANT
45cm (18in) high

POT SIZE
12cm (5in)

Schlechterara Blue Boy 'Indigo' AM/AOS

Many hybrids within the *Vanda* alliance exhibit the lovely blue colour which is so welcome here and so rare in other orchids. Only the vandas have provided the orchid world with the fantastic colour range which extends from the palest sky blue to the vibrant colour seen in this clone. The parents of the acclaimed American bigeneric hybrid, raised in 1967, are *Ascocenda* Meda Arnold and *Vanda coerulea*. Here the *Vanda*, which appears twice in its parentage, has become the dominant parent, the *Ascocenda* having had little influence. Outside the tropical regions of the world, the warm-loving vandas can be sluggish to reach their full potential, or to bloom when required. Grown with such ease in places like Florida and Thailand, they represent a greater challenge in less sunny climes, but one which orchid lovers embrace.

FLOWER
5cm (2in) wide

FLOWER SPIKE
30cm (12in) long

PLANT
45cm (18in) high

POT SIZE
12cm (5in)

Vandanthe Varavuth

FLOWER
5cm (2in) wide

FLOWER SPIKE
15cm (6in) long

PLANT
30cm (12in) high

POT SIZE
12cm (5in)

The beautiful Varavuth, raised in Thailand and grown wherever sufficient light can be given for it to bloom successfully, produces exquisite light blue flowers on upright flower spikes. Their colour is similar to the delicate pigments of the blue Burmese species *Vanda coerulea* from which so many of today's hybrids have been raised. In addition to the fabled blue, seldom found in any other orchid, the vandas may be almost any colour or combination of colours which are unique to the genus. Varavuth is both warm- and cool-tolerant, growing well in both tropical and temperate climates.

Vanda Violeta 'Fuchs Sky' HCC/AOS

The brilliantly coloured flowers of this *Vanda* have large, rounded petals and sepals with a diminutive lip, an unusual feature among the more popular types of orchid. Their colouring is distinctly mottled, or tessellated, over the whole flower. The blooms open a slatey blue and take several days to mature and gain their true blue colouring. Originally raised in Britain in 1959 by David Sander's Orchids, the primary hybrid between *V. tessellata* and *V. coerulea* has been recently remade in the USA, using superior, nursery-bred clones of *V. coerulea* and has become a building block for future generations. These orchids are high light lovers and grow best in tropical countries of the Far East, where they bloom freely, often several times a year, and where most of the hybridizing is done. In temperate climates they are less free-flowering and the lack of year-round sunshine restricts their growth, which makes vandas a challenging prospect for specialized growers.

FLOWER
9cm (3¹/2in) wide

FLOWER SPIKE
20cm (8in) long

PLANT
45cm (18in) high

POT SIZE
12cm (5in)

Vandanthe Memoria Lyle Swanson 'Justin Grannel'

This superb clone typifies all that is outstanding about vandas, an impressive genus in which can be found the richest colours of any orchid. The blooms are carried on upright flower spikes, their large size and rounded shape causing each bloom to overlap the next, creating a wonderfully dense sphere of bold, vibrant colour. Through generations of breeding the natural hues have been intensified and improved, along with the flower shape. The intense violet-purple shown here is made up of several layers of colour, one on top of the other. It can be traced back to, among others, the species *V. tessellata*, whose tessellated petals can be seen to have influenced this clone, raised in 1991 by Robert Fuchs in Florida.

FLOWER
9cm (3¹/2in) wide

FLOWER SPIKE
30cm (12in) long

PLANT
45cm (18in) high

POT SIZE
12cm (5in)

Vanda cristata

An attractive *Vanda*, this is a cool-growing, high-altitude species first introduced from Nepal in 1818. It was sent to the Royal Botanic Gardens at Kew and described in 1834. It has long been appreciated for its ease of cultivation and willingness to bloom regularly and freely, in Britain as well as elsewhere in the temperate world, during the summer and autumn months. Its delightful little flowers with their clear green petals and sepals and the strangely formed lip, white with red streaks, make it popular in mixed collections. The flowers are carried on short spikes which come from the axils between the leaves. The plant is compact, producing light green leaves in pairs; though a well-cultivated plant can grow quite tall, it seldom becomes top-heavy.

GROWERS' TIP
Grow between 10°C (50°F) min. and 30°C (85°F) max. for best results.

FLOWER
2cm (1in) wide

FLOWER SPIKE
5cm (2in) long

PLANT
15cm (6in) high

POT SIZE
8cm (3in)

Vanda suavis

This variable species was originally discovered in Java in 1846 by Thomas Lobb, one of the famous Lobb brothers who was collecting for Veitch. Though grown less widely than the more colourful hybrids which are so plentiful today, it produces distinctively shaped and coloured flowers, with a dozen or more on the stem. The species can vary in colouring from creamy white to yellow, with reddish or brown heavy spotting; the illustration shows a particularly well-coloured form. The curiously shaped lip, an attractive part of the flower, may vary from blue-mauve to red-brown. *V. suavis* blooms during the autumn and winter, and is both long-lasting and fragrant. The plant, which carries its long, semi-rigid leaves in pairs along an ever-extending rhizome, can become extremely tall but may be reduced by cutting the rhizome in half to produce two plants. This may only be done, however, if each piece can be left with sufficient aerial roots to maintain a new plant.

FLOWER
5cm (2in) wide

FLOWER SPIKE
30cm (12in) long

PLANT
90cm (36in) high

POT SIZE
30cm (12in)

Calanthe Prinsesse Alexandra

FLOWER
4cm (1¹/2in) wide

FLOWER SPIKE
70cm (28in) long

PLANT
60cm (24in) high

POT SIZE
12cm (5in)

This new hybrid, raised in Denmark and registered in 1997, is the result of crossing the species *C. rosea* with a modern hybrid, *C.* Grouville. The flower exhibits many of the characteristics of the species, with its light pink, soft-textured blooms on a long, arching flower spike. The flowers last for many weeks over the winter period, with the spike extending to provide a succession of blooms. The plant needs to be grown in warm conditions during the summer to accommodate its fast-growing habit. The silver-grey pseudobulbs do not live as long as in other orchids, and will have shrivelled and died after two years, leaving only the newest one to grow and perpetuate the plant. When repotting the plant in spring, divide the pseudobulbs singly and place them together in one large pot for best effect.

Christieara Renée Gerber 'Fuchs Confetti' HCC/AOS

This trigeneric hybrid, raised in 1990 by Robert Fuchs, combines the qualities of *Aerides*, *Ascocentrum* and *Vanda*. The colourful, spotted flowers are waxy in texture, with a distinctive lip, inherited from *Aerides lawrenceana*, which has also given the plant its fragrance and modified the flower's overall shape. The flower spike, with numerous blooms, is held in an arching spray. The plant is more compact and may grow a little cooler than other hybrids in this group. See page 56 for another illustration.

FLOWER
5cm (2in) wide

FLOWER SPIKE
30cm (12in) long

PLANT
45cm (18in) high

POT SIZE
12cm (5in)

Cultivation

The majority of orchids are epiphytic plants which are used to an aerial lifestyle, and their roots have evolved accordingly. Even though the hybrids may be many times removed from the species through generations of breeding, they retain the same basic plant and root structure of these original species, which is what makes the culture of orchids different from that of most other plants.

Compost

What constitutes a good compost for epiphytic orchids has been debated since the plants were first cultivated over 200 years ago. Since experimentation with various substances is ongoing, orchid composts are continually being monitored and improved. Cultural practices also vary around the world, as materials available in one country may be unobtainable elsewhere.

The first requirement of an orchid compost is that it should be open, well-aerated and free-draining. In addition it needs to hold the plant steady in its pot and should retain enough moisture and nutrients for long-term absorption by the roots. It must also be slow to decompose, reasonably easy and pleasant to use and readily available. The most widely used organic material which fits all these attributes is pine bark chippings. This compost is available through most of the orchid-growing world, generally in fine and coarse grades. It consists of the bark chippings from commercially raised and cropped pine trees which, in Europe, is likely to be Scots or Corsican pine and in the USA redwood cedar.

There are several variations on this bark-based compost. For example, a proportion of peat may be added, increasing its moisture-holding qualities, which is an advantage for some orchids with thick rooting systems, such as *Cymbidium* and *Zygopetalum*. It is also useful for busy growers who may be unable to tend to the watering of their plants often, and need them to stay wet for longer periods. Other organic materials that can be used as a substitue for peat include beech husks, coir and tree fern fibre.

A number of man-made materials make good, if unlikely, orchid composts. These include materials such as Rockwool and horticultural foam, both of which are artificially made fibres with all the qualities looked for in a good compost, except that they are inert and cannot therefore contribute any nutrients to the plant. The advantages of these types of material are that the plant can be kept much wetter without any danger of infection or rot setting in and, as there is no slow decomposition, the compound does not alter over the years. The disadvantage is that it becomes necessary to supply the plants with exactly the right amount of feed in a balanced combination to maintain steady growth. It is best to use this type of compost only after gaining some experience using the more traditional organic bark.

Two types of Rockwool are available, absorbent and water-repellant. They can be mixed together or used separately, depending on the degree of moisture retention needed.

A number of other inert materials are suitable for orchids, used on their own or combined with a bark and peat mixture: these include horticultural foam and expanded clay pellets. These materials are absorbent, help to retain moisture and allow air to circulate around the roots.

Any potting material should be soaked beforehand and used in a dampened state. Bone-dry compost is difficult to work with and will take a long time to absorb water in the pot, which could harm the newly potted plant by retarding the growth of its new roots. When using man-made materials, it can be harmful to inhale the dust particles, which is another reason to dampen them; by the same token you should wear disposable gloves when handling these materials. Mix only enough compost for your immediate needs because, if

stored damp, the organic mixes will encourage the growth of moulds which can change the material's acidity.

When deciding on the best compost for your orchids, be advised by the nursery that supplied them. Try to keep all your orchids in the same type of mix, but if after some time a particular plant is not doing well, consider changing to another compost. However, you should avoid constantly changing composts in the hope of reviving an ailing plant, as the underlying cause of its ill health may lie elsewhere and continually disturbing its roots will make matters worse. Never mix an organic compost with inert material when repotting: do not, for example, fill around a Rockwool-planted orchid with bark compost, as the two have different cultural requirements and are not compatible.

Watering

Orchids are slow-growing plants, many living for years following a regulated pattern of growing and resting cycles. While the plants are growing they need to be kept evenly moist

ABOVE
Shown above are several alternative orchid composts. Bark chippings come in three grades (centre, left and rear), while the man-made alternatives include horticultural foam, an inert mix of foam sponge and dried moss (front), and Rockwool (far right).

LEFT
Most orchids will do well potted in an organic compost like bark chippings, which is both free-draining and slow to decompose.

If your orchids are in a modern inert material, such as Rockwool, there is far less danger of roots rotting, and they can safely be kept in a perpetually wet state without the risk of overwatering.

Plants that have suffered underwatering over a long period will simply stop growing roots and those in the pot will eventually dry up and die. Once the root system is prevented from taking up water for storage in the pseudobulbs, these will shrivel as reserves are used up. Shrivelled pseudobulbs can therefore be the result of either underwatering or overwatering, but a close look at the state of the compost in the pot will quickly determine the likely cause of the problem. While the underwatered plant will recover after a good soak, one which has been overwatered will need careful repotting and attention over a much longer period before it recovers fully.

The amount of water to give at one application varies according to the individual plant. A plant which has filled its pot with a solid rootball or has pushed itself out of the pot will be difficult to water because most of what is poured on will run off over the edge of the pot. If only a little penetrates the compost, it may appear wet on the top but still be dry underneath. This is especially true of the thick-rooting cymbidiums, which can become potbound after a couple of years, when underwatering becomes a risk.

A newly potted plant, on the other hand, surrounded by fresh compost and with a less developed root system, can easily be overwatered if the same amount were to be poured onto it. Water a newly potted plant by flooding the surface several times until it retains enough water to soak right through to the bottom of the pot. The smaller the pot, the

at the roots, without the compost becoming either too wet or too dry. The open nature of orchid compost should ensure that water drains through the pot within seconds, retaining just enough for the roots to absorb.

Watering probably causes more concern to the beginner than any other aspect of growing orchids as the unfamiliar pseudobulbs and unusual compost do not make it clear when the orchid is in need of water. While the surface of the compost may look dry it can be quite wet underneath. Lifting the plant to test whether it feels light is a good way of deciding and if you are still unsure, weigh the plants on the kitchen scales!

Both overwatering and underwatering can cause problems. If too much water stays in the compost for too long, an organic medium such as bark will stagnate and decompose, causing the valuable slow-growing roots to die from lack of air. Each pseudobulb develops its own roots at the start of the growing season and the plant will have to survive on these until the next new growths are active and can produce their own roots. Older pseudobulbs which have lost their roots are unlikely to make new ones again and will simply shrivel.

more often it will require watering and in a greenhouse those plants standing closest to the ventilators or the heater will dry out more rapidly.

The best way to water orchids is from the top, using a long-spouted can and pouring water over and all around the surface of the compost. With newly repotted orchids growing in a bark mixture, take care not to wash the bark pieces over the rim of the pot. It will do no harm to splash water onto the mature pseudobulbs, allowing the water to run down between them, but make sure you do not get water into the funnel of a growing pseudobulb, or the centre leaf of a monopodial orchid such as *Paphiopedilum*. Water lodging in any of these places can cause basal rot.

The easiest means of watering orchids grown in the home is to take the plants into the kitchen, where you can water them on the draining board and return them to their growing area after surplus water has drained away. In this way you avoid the danger of orchids being left standing in a saucer of water, which stops them drying out evenly and can be detrimental to the roots. If the orchids are to be watered in situ, stand them on upturned saucers or half-pots in a tray deep enough for surplus water not to spill onto the floor.

The best time to water your orchids is while the temperature is rising. In the summer, and on warm, sunny days this can be at any time of day, but in winter water only in the morning. By the time the temperature starts to drop in late afternoon or evening, all surplus water should have dried up. In summer, much more water will be needed because the plants are actively growing and transpiring more, while some water will be lost to evaporation.

Try to check your plants almost daily: you will probably need to water about once or twice a week, depending on the state of the compost. In winter, some orchids will be resting, while others will simply be growing more slowly. Slow-growing orchids need to be kept just slightly moist, so water them occasionally. Those that are resting need just enough water to prevent the pseudobulbs from shrivelling – or none at all.

Epiphytic orchids growing on bark rafts should be sprayed once or twice a day through most of the year to keep them in a moist state. In addition you should dunk them in a bucket of water two or three times a week to ensure they stay moist. When a plant is growing on bark, and has a good aerial root system, it is almost impossible to overwater it, as there is nowhere for a quantity of water to remain.

BELOW
To water your orchids in situ, stand them on an upturned saucer, or similar, in a tray deep enough to contain any water that may drain through.

But it can easily be underwatered, in which case the pseudobulbs will start to shrivel and the aerial roots will stop growing.

When you submerge a plant in water, be careful not to damage the growing tips of the roots, especially of vandas and other thick, semi-rigid, rooting orchids. It may be easier to fill a large, shallow tray with water and lie the plant down with its bark and roots soaking, while the leaves remain above water. The roots of aerial orchids will adhere to their immediate surroundings, making it impossible to remove the plant from the bark without breaking the roots. Where orchids have been established on a fixed tree branch, water them through a rose, heavily enough to penetrate the compost around the bark. Since this method is not remotely practical in the house, aerial growing is really best confined to either the greenhouse or the conservatory.

Use water at room temperature for orchids growing indoors. Orchids prefer soft water and, if this is not available, you can convert hard water by placing a muslin bag, or a length of nylon stocking, filled with peat in the water storage butt. This can be left in permanently over a long period before it needs to be replaced. The water will turn slightly brown from the leaching of the peat but this will not harm the orchids. Water used for creating humidity can be used straight from the mains, but you should avoid spraying the plants with hard, scaly water which may leave a coating of limescale over the leaves.

Feeding

In the wild, epiphytic orchids are deluged with water daily throughout their growing season. Drying winds and the sun that follows heavy rain ensure they are soon dry again. With each

downpour, water is washed down the bark of the trees bringing with it meagre nutrients in the form of bird or animal droppings and decomposing leaf litter which can settle around the roots and at the base of the orchids. In this way the plants receive additional nourishment, but they remain essentially light feeders.

In cultivation you must apply artificial feed according to the type of compost. The traditional mixture using bark chippings as a base gives a slowly decomposing material, releasing a steady food supply over a long period which, in itself, is sufficient for some orchids. Those growing in more modern inorganic, man-made fibres are totally dependent on feed administered to the pot for their nourishment. Both materials have their advantages, but in the inert composts you can be more certain of getting the feeding exactly right, whereas with the organic compost you can never be sure just how much a plant is benefitting from decomposition. It is an advantage to your orchids to feed them lightly as more harm can generally be done through overfeeding, which causes the roots to be burnt by an over-supply of chemicals building up in the compost.

Balanced orchid feed is available in liquid or granular form through specialized nurseries and garden centres. The liquid feed comes in concentrated form and the recommended dosage often requires it to be diluted into litres of water so that, if you only have a few plants, far too much has to made up at a time. Do not be tempted to re-use the rest of this amount over a long period – a new solution should be mixed for each feeding and any remainder simply discarded. In the same way a bottle of liquid feed should not be kept for more than one season as it may change its chemical composition slightly over a period of time. Granular feed has the advantage that it can be made up in smaller quantities, which is easier for the small indoor collection, with none going to waste.

Orchid feed can be nitrate- or phosphate-based. Nitrate-based feeds are used to promote growth and should be applied to a plant at the start of its growing season and continued until its growth is fully developed. Phosphate-based feeds are used to encourage flowering in a plant which has completed its growing. Once the pseudobulb is forming and maturing, but before the flower spikes are visible, discontinue the nitrate-based feed and apply phosphate-based feed right through the flowering season, following the rhythm of the seasons without being hurried; do not attempt to force a plant into flowering before its time.

Orchids need feeding only while they are growing and active, but the start of the growing season may vary, depending on the orchid. Begin feeding as soon as the new growth is seen to be active, with new roots at the base, and continue throughout the summer months, gradually lessening during the autumn; discontinue feeding by the onset of winter. Once the growing season is over and the plant is resting, or has slowed down its growth in response to the change of season, you should discontinue the application of feed for any deciduous orchids, such as *Lycaste* or *Calanthe*, and reduce it for *Cymbidium* and *Odontoglossum*.

The best way to apply feed is to water the solution into the pot, directly from the top. In some circumstances it is more practical to spray the foliage and aerial roots where these are growing freely. Only healthy orchids should be given feed – sick plants which have lost their roots have no means of taking up the extra nutrients and any feed will remain unused, eventually souring the compost and destroying any new roots which later appear.

Always apply feed when the compost is moist, before a plant dries out. Adding feed to a dry pot can prevent it dispersing properly, which again can damage the roots. Orchids that are otherwise healthy, but whose foliage has a yellowish colour, may be suffering from a lack of nutrients, and in this case it can be beneficial to spray the foliage lightly with diluted feed to restore it to a good healthy green. This is also a good way of feeding a plant which has lost its roots but which still has plenty of foliage.

There is no need to apply feed every time a plant is watered. To prevent the build-up of unwanted salts in the compost, give at least one good watering with clear water in between each feed application. This will flush the compost and ensure that all unwanted fertilizer is washed through.

Orchids that are resting should not be given artificial food until they are growing well. This also applies to small divisions and newly potted plants, all of which need to make their own roots before they can take advantage of the extra nutrients.

Spraying

Spraying orchids is not a substitute for watering but an additional part of their care; it should become a daily routine. In the home, you can spray the plants with a hand-held bottle spray, wetting the foliage just enough to allow small droplets of water to remain on the leaves, but not so much that the surplus runs down them to create problems inside the new growths, or the central leaves on *Phalaenopsis* and *Paphiopedilum*. Lightly mist all parts of the plant, including underneath and around the base tray. During the summer this will help to cool the foliage as well as keeping the leaves dust-free. Where orchids are grown in a greenhouse, spraying is even more important to aid respiration during hot weather. Spray at least once a day in the morning in summer, increasing this during spells of hot weather; during the winter months restrict spraying to warm, sunny days.

Evergreen orchids such as *Cymbidium*, *Odontoglossum* and *Cattleya* can be liberally sprayed for most of the year, while deciduous kinds, including *Calanthe*, *Lycaste* and *Pleione*, should hardly be sprayed at all – their softer foliage will become spotted if water is allowed to lie on it for several hours at a time. A light misting on sunny days is sufficient.

In the greenhouse spraying can be used to create a humid atmosphere. Drenching the floor and staging on a daily basis will maintain humidity and help to achieve an atmosphere consistent with good growing conditions. Use a hosepipe with a lance attached as a much greater quantity of water will be used.

LEFT
Spray orchid leaves lightly with water on a regular basis to keep them fresh and free from dust.

RIGHT
Keep a humidity tray filled with pebbles topped up with water to create a moist microclimate.

Humidity

Humidity is synonymous with good orchid culture. It is not to be confused with spraying or watering, but helps to provide the right background atmosphere in which your orchids can grow. The surrounding humidity should always balance the temperature as far as possible. In the greenhouse, regular damping down – which entails soaking the area where the orchids are growing – should be carried out more in summer and less in winter when temperatures are low and the light poor. In summer, damp down in the morning, as the temperature is rising, repeating it on hot days at midday or early in the afternoon. As the temperature cools towards evening, the humidity will rise automatically, by which time the foliage and surface water should already have evaporated, and you may not need to put down more water until the following day. On rainy days there will be enough humidity without any damping down.

Indoors there is little humidity available, but this aspect of orchid growing becomes less important where the temperature fluctuates less. The more constant temperature within the home creates a different atmosphere and, provided plants are kept evenly moist at the roots while they are growing, they will not suffer from lack of humidity. Some orchids, such as *Phalaenopsis*, are less prone to fungal attacks in the home. Where the orchids are standing on humidity trays filled with pebbles or expanded clay pellets and topped up with water, there will be sufficient moisture rising up to create a microclimate. Indoor growing cases can be fitted with humidity trays in the same way. Humidity becomes significantly more important indoors in winter, when central heating dries the air faster, so spraying to maintain humidity can continue throughout most of the year.

In a conservatory, where it is most difficult to achieve the balance between humidity and temperature, orchids should be sprayed vigilantly and humidity trays used where possible.

Light and shade

Orchids need light but not full sun. Their leaves have adapted over millions of years to thrive in the dappled shade provided by the tree canopy of their natural home.

In the home or greenhouse, aim to keep the foliage a good healthy green, avoiding any stress to the plants caused by too much light. In a greenhouse the light comes in from all around and you will need to shade the glass during spring and summer, using a paint or cloth

shading or a combination of both. As a rough guide it should be possible to glance at the sun through the shading without it hurting your eyes. The amount of shade should not reduce the light so much that the greenhouse becomes gloomy, and how much shade is put on will depend greatly on its siting. If there are large trees outside, these will provide much natural shade, here shade cloth should be enough to keep down the summer temperature.

In the home light usually enters a room from one direction only, so there is little danger of the orchids becoming exposed to too much light unless they are standing directly in the sun close to a south-facing window. Here shade can easily be provided by net curtains, slatted blinds or an outside sun blind. Provided the sun is not shining directly onto the foliage at midday in the summer, most orchids can benefit from the early morning or late afternoon and evening sun, when the rays will reach the leaves at an angle low enough not to harm them. Some orchids, like *Cymbidium*, *Dendrobium* and *Coelogyne*, can take more direct light than others. *Phalaenopsis* and *Paphiopedilum* require the most shade, and these should always be kept further away from the window, or stood behind other plants

which will afford them extra shade. Cattleyas are often thought of as tolerating high light levels, but they can suffer more than most from direct sun, which may quickly burn into their fleshy leaves.

In winter, in the greenhouse as well as in the home, give the orchids all the light available. The most dangerous time of the year is early spring as the sun is gaining in power daily, and the orchids, having not been exposed to bright sun all winter, can suffer from too much light coming in too quickly; it is as well to put some shading in position during this time.

Orchids grown in the home can be given separate summer and winter quarters to take into account the light they receive. While a south- or west-facing aspect may be ideal in winter, this would give too much sun in summer. Either move the orchids to an east- or north-facing window for the summer, or leave them where they are if shading is provided. Here again, outside trees or hedging may provide partial shade. In the summer, place a thermometer near the glass where the orchids are to give an accurate temperature reading, which can be several degrees higher than it is a little further into the room.

Orchids exposed to too much light or direct sun will show stress by their leaves turning yellowish or reddish, and if the sun burns a leaf this will appear as a black or brown area on the surface directly facing the sun. Those which have been kept too heavily shaded or in a poorly lit area of the home will look dramatically different from healthy orchids. Their foliage will be darker green, lacking lustre or gloss. The leaves will be long and lank and the pseudobulbs will not have ripened sufficiently to produce a flower spike.

Temperature

For cultivation purposes, orchids are neatly divided into three main groups of temperature tolerance, depending on where the original species originate in the wild. The altitude at which the orchids are found is more important than their global position, and whether they grow high in the tree canopy or near the base of the tree in leaf litter.

It is quite natural, indeed essential, for orchids to experience fluctuations of temperature from day to day. A comfortable temperature range between which orchids can be grown is from 10–30°C (50–86°F), a range which encompasses the various requirements of all the cultivated orchids, with the exception of *Pleione* and a few others which need a cooler, but still frost-free, winter home.

Although the occasional hot day or cold night will not harm them, if orchids are exposed to extremes of temperature over a long period, their performance will be affected and their growth will slow until it ceases altogether. By the end of their growing season a much smaller pseudobulb or growth will have been produced and premature leaf loss will occur. Orchids exposed to below recommended temperatures during the winter will take longer to produce new growths in spring and will also suffer from leaf loss. Cool-growing orchids which are kept too warm in the summer will respond by not flowering, though their growth may appear to be normal.

Most of the orchids in cultivation are cool-growing, including *Cymbidium, Coelogyne* and many more. Cool-growing orchids (pages 58–123) require a minimum night temperature of 10°C (50°F) and a maximum summer temperature of 24°C (75°F). Intermediate orchids (pages 124–169) need a winter minimum temperature of 13°C (55°F), with a summer daytime maximum of 30°C (86°F), and the warm-growing orchids (pages 170–197) should have a minimum winter night temperature of 18°C (64°F), with a summer daytime maximum of 32°C (90°F). Where orchids from all three groups grow in different areas of the home or greenhouse, the main difference in temperature will be at night in the winter. During summer there will be little variation between daytime temperatures, which are dependent on natural conditions.

To maintain high enough temperatures in winter, artificial heating will generally be needed. In a greenhouse this will be supplied by a heater; for orchids electric heating is the safest and most efficient. A conservatory can easily be heated by running an extra radiator from the central heating system in the house. Do not keep cool-growing orchids too warm at night as this will affect their flower production; the same problem will occur if intermediate or warm-growing orchids are kept too cold.

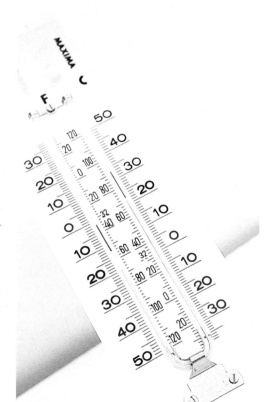

LEFT
A maximum/minimum thermometer is one of the most important pieces of equipment you can have. This will record the rise and fall in temperature when you are away, or at night.

Repotting and dividing

Adult orchids are generally repotted every two years in spring, at the start of their growing season. Repotting involves removing the plant from its pot and discarding all old compost, trimming the roots and returning it to a larger pot with fresh compost. Young seedlings and divisions need to be kept moving and are 'dropped on' every six months in spring and early autumn. Dropping on is when a young plant is carefully taken from one pot and placed into a larger one without any disturbance to the rootball; it is used when the existing compost does not need replacing. When repotting an orchid that has outgrown its pot, you may wish to consider dividing it to form several new plants, rather than simply increasing the pot size.

A plant is in need of repotting when the compost has deteriorated and is clogged with decomposing particles. If you can push a finger through the compost, this indicates that it has largely broken down, has no food value left and is no longer aerated. Left in this compost, a plant will quickly lose its roots as water does not drain through and the compost becomes sodden. Plants also need repotting when there is no room for further growth to be made within the pot, or when the roots have become so cramped that the plant has pushed itself above the rim. A further reason is when a plant has become sick through incorrect watering and needs urgent attention to its roots. Do not repot orchids which are flowering or resting, but wait until the new growth shows.

The aim of every orchid grower is to keep the plants in harmony and balance which, in the case of evergreen sympodial orchids, is when there are several pseudobulbs in full leaf. As these age, they naturally shed their leaves,

usually one or two in a season, until none are left, at which stage the pseudobulb is termed a back bulb. Back bulbs retain food reserves and can be propagated to make new plants when an inactive eye at the base is encouraged to grow (see page 216). A plant should always have more pseudobulbs in leaf than out of leaf but where, over a period, several have lost their foliage, you should cut off all surplus back bulbs, otherwise they can restrict the new growth and successive pseudobulbs will start to get smaller.

Deciduous sympodial orchids such as *Lycaste* and *Anguloa* are different because they shed all or most of their season's foliage at one time. While some do this at the start of winter when they enter their dormant state, others retain most of their leaves until spring, discarding them just before coming into new growth and flowering. These orchids can easily support up to four to six leafless pseudobulbs, but the plant size does need to be reduced once successive pseudobulbs start to become smaller rather than increasing or remaining the same size.

Orchids which produce more than one new growth, or lead, will grow in different directions at once and these plants can be divided (see pages 214–215) provided that at least four pseudobulbs, mostly in leaf, can be left on each division. Never divide a plant into pieces smaller than four pseudobulbs each or you will prevent it from flowering for at least another year. You can of course leave plants intact if you are growing them on into specimen size, provided there are always more pseudobulbs with leaves to keep the balance. The pseudobulbs are attached by a strong rhizome which is usually below the surface and not easily visible except in cattleyas and similar

types. Monopodial orchids do not extend outwards to fill their pots but need repotting when the compost has deteriorated, or when they have been in the same pot for more than two years. Tall-growing vandas and similar orchids can become top-heavy and by the time their pots are full of roots they need to be placed in a larger container. Shorter-growing monopodials, in particular *Phalaenopsis*, are mostly dropped on to avoid disturbing their roots. Where decomposed compost has to be replaced, the plants are usually returned to the same size pot.

Repotting phalaenopsis

Orchids which have a number of aerial roots outside the pot can be repotted in the same way as cymbidiums, but without placing the aerial roots in the compost (see above right). Having developed in the air, they would suffocate and die if transferred to the container. Repot carefully so as not to break the aerial roots and leave them outside the pot. Give the plants a few days to allow damaged or bruised roots to heal, then water sparingly; resume normal watering a week later. Spray the leaves often to reduce moisture lost through foliage.

Repotting upward-creeping orchids

Many epiphytic orchids develop an upward-creeping habit, producing each pseudobulb slightly above the previous one. This can make repotting difficult where there is also an extensive mass of aerial roots. Here the older pseudobulbs may be buried deeper in the pot to bring the new growth level with the rim. Alternatively, insert a mossy pole or length of palm fibre into the pot, on to which the plant can grow. It will soon attach itself by new roots and continue to grow upward with the extra support. If the plant becomes top-heavy, place a few weighty stones in the base of the pot to stop it toppling over.

Repotting cymbidiums

Before you start, lay down a few sheets of newspaper to collect the old compost and roots which are to be discarded. Have ready a supply of dampened compost, preferably wetted the previous day, a selection of larger-size pots and a supply of crocking material for drainage. This can be pieces of polystyrene used for packing or broken polystyrene tiles. You will also need a pair of scissors, secateurs or a sharp pruning knife; these tools should be sterilized, so have a cigarette lighter or a bottle of methylated spirits handy and flame or clean the tool after each use. It is a good idea to wear disposable gloves if you are using a man-made fibre such as Rockwool or horticultural foam. And if you plan to divide some plants at the same time as repotting, have a few spare labels and a waterproof pen to hand.

1 Remove the orchid from its pot by holding it upside down and tapping the edge of the pot against the worktop. If the plant is not too rootbound it will slide out easily.

GROWERS' TIP
Where a plant is rootbound and there is a thick ball of roots, run the pruning knife around the inside rim to loosen them.

2 Lay the plant on the newspaper and examine its roots: they should be white and firm to the touch, with active growing tips. Remove any which are blackened and hollow. The dead roots may be wet and soggy or, if they have been dead for a long time, they will have dried out and the outer covering will pull away to reveal the inner wire-like core. Cut away any of these dead roots using secateurs, after teasing the roots apart. If all the roots look white and healthy and the plant is not to be divided, you can simply slip it into a pot about 5cm (2in) larger.

GROWERS' TIP
If there are many dead roots, the compost will fall away as you work.

3 First place a layer of crocks at the bottom of the pot and, if room allows, add some compost. Place the orchid on top of this, with the oldest pseudobulbs against one side of the pot, allowing as much space as possible between the new growths and the rim: this is the direction in which the plant will continue to grow.

4 Hold the plant firmly so that the base of the new growth is level with the top of the pot and pour compost all around the plant and push in with your fingers by pressing down against the rim of the pot until it is steady in the pot. The pseudobulbs should 'sit' comfortably on the surface, 2.5cm (1in) from the top of the container, to allow for watering the plant without washing compost over the edge. If the plant is standing too high it will not be firm enough, and if potted too deep the base of the new growth will be below the level of the compost, which could lead to rotting.

Dividing coelogynes

1 When repotting a larger plant which needs dividing or its back bulbs reducing, remove it from the pot and decide where to divide it. You can divide a large plant into several pieces, but each useable piece should be no smaller than four pseudobulbs. Push the pseudobulbs apart with your fingers and thumb where you intend to make the split and, using a pruning knife, sever the rhizome in between the pseudobulbs. Continue to cut through the rootball until the two parts are separated.

2 Remove all old or decayed compost from the main part of the plant, then tease out the roots, trimming back all broken, cut and dead ones with secateurs or scissors to the base of the plant. Trim the live roots to a length of about 15cm (6in). Orchids do not make permanent roots and this allows more space in the pot for them to grow.

3 Having been reduced in size, the main portion of the plant may be returned to the same size pot, or possibly one slightly larger, making sure there is a 5cm (2in) gap for it to grow into. Hold the plant firmly and fill in around with compost: because much of the rootball has been cut away, more compost will be needed to fill the space and it must be firmed down to hold the plant steady. If the plant is loose in its pot at this stage, it will not produce new roots into the compost.

4 Where a plant is divided into equal portions, repot the other divisions in the same way, using a pot of the right size.

Leafless back bulbs that have been removed will have no live roots, these having died naturally when the leaves were shed. If you wish to use back bulbs for propagating (see page 216), divide them up singly, reserving those which are plump and green. Trim back the dead roots, leaving just enough to anchor each bulb, and pot them into separate small pots or round the edge of a community pot. The older, shrivelled back bulbs will have insufficient reserves left to be expected to grow, so they can be discarded.

GROWERS' TIP
When cutting through the rhizome, be careful to avoid slicing into the fleshy pseudobulbs.

GROWERS' TIP
By trimming back long straggly roots you are helping to stimulate new root production.

GROWERS' TIP
Cutting a Cattleya's rhizome in autumn encourages the back pseudobulbs to grow. By spring both divisions should be showing new growth.

GROWERS' TIP
Remove basal new growths when they have made roots and pot separately.

Repotting and dividing cattleyas

Prior to dividing and repotting a *Cattleya*, cut the rhizome in autumn while still in the pot. Repot in the spring, once a new growth appears on the back portion.

Repotting and dividing slipper orchids

Repot these orchids as for cymbidiums (see page 212). Divide large enough plants so that each division has at least four growths with a new, developing shoot visible. Remove back growths for propagating once the plant is out of its pot by severing them with a pruning knife.

Repotting and dividing vandas

Orchids like *Vanda*, which make thickened aerial roots, are best potted in slatted baskets to allow air around the base. Divide tall vandas horizontally when large enough to leave the top with plenty of aerial roots and the bottom with leaves and roots. Leave young growths until they have their own root system and at least six pairs of leaves. Stanhopeas also need to be potted in open baskets to provide an exit for their subterranean flower spikes.

Vegetative propagation

Propagating orchids is a slow process, often taking several years for a new plant to flower, and is only worth considering with your best plants. However, bringing on your own propagated plants can be a challenge for the orchid grower and is worth a try for favourite orchids that you wish to duplicate.

Sympodial orchids are propagated by removing the leafless back bulbs from the main plant at repotting time and potting them up on their own (see page 214). Back bulbs which are to be propagated must not be too old or shrivelled but robust and plump, with one or more spare eyes at their base. Cymbidiums are among the easiest orchids to grow from back bulbs and will take three to four years to flower. Most orchids can be propagated from back bulbs, although some grow more readily than others. Odontoglossums, for example, rarely succeed in the usual way.

Monopodial orchids are less easy to propagate, although *Vanda* and *Phalaenopsis* will occasionally produce a new plant naturally and can be encouraged to do so. Vandas may produce new growths from their base, particularly if the centre has been damaged and is unable to grow. *Phalaenopsis* occasionally produce keikis, or young plants, from the ends of their flowering stems. Hybrids of *Phalaenopsis lueddemanniana* in particular will readily produce a number of these growths from one stem. While these methods of propagation are not as reliable as that for sympodial orchids, it is fun to try if you want to increase your stock.

Propagating from a back bulb

1 The dormant eye found at the base of a *Cymbidium* back bulb is protected by a brown, triangular bract which becomes visible once you know what to look for. (In *Cattleya* the dormant eyes are green and particularly prominent.) Gently scrape away the outer covering to reveal greenish white tissue underneath before potting up the back bulb; if the tissue is black, the eye is dead and will not grow.

2 Once potted, place the back bulbs in a small propagating frame and keep warm and moist. A soil-warming unit and moisture tray will further encourage new growth, which should appear within six weeks. When a new growth is several centimetres high, remove it from the propagator to a growing area and allow it to develop further. Repot at six-monthly intervals until a pseudobulb is formed, then grow on as an adult plant.

Propagating dendrobiums (pictured)

Propagate the soft-caned *D. nobile* type in spring by removing an older, leafless cane and cutting it into sections in between the nodes from where the leaves were shed.

Dust the pieces with sulphur powder at both ends, look for the slightly swollen nodes where sections are joined and bury upright up to a node in a container of potting material.

Alternatively, lay stem lengths on their sides in a seedling tray. In a few months you will see healthy growth emerging from a node.

With the hard-caned *D. phalaenopsis* type of *Dendrobium*, only the top portion of the older canes have dormant eyes. To propagate, remove this part and pot up.

Propagating cattleyas

Sever the rhizome while the plant is in the pot during autumn, (see page 215). By the following spring the severed pseudobulb will have started a new growth. Remove this and pot up separately from the main plant.

Propagating vandas

Encourage new growth by wrapping the plant in foam rubber around the stem and tying it in place. Keep moist and remove occasionally to check for new growth. At this stage, remove the wrapping and spray regularly as a new plantlet forms. When this has grown its own roots and leaves, sever it and pot it separately.

Propagating phalaenopsis

To encourage a keiki (young plant) to develop, coat the nodes along the stem with keiki paste (obtained from specialty nurseries). In time a new plant complete with its own roots, may start to grow. At this stage remove the new plantlet from its parent and pot it separately.

GROWERS' TIP
Use a sharp knife or secateurs to cut the leafless Dendrobium nobile cane into suitable-sized pieces.

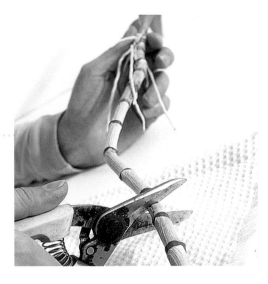

GROWERS' TIP
Dusting the ends with sulphur powder stops the pieces rotting.

GROWERS' TIP
Burying the cut pieces up to a node allows new growth to develop on the surface of the potting mix.

Resting

In their natural state orchids cease growing during the dry season and hibernate in response to lack of moisture. After completing their season's growth during the summer rainy season, the mature pseudobulbs store enough reserves of water and nutrients to carry the plants through the forthcoming drought. In cultivation orchids continue to follow this cycle of growing and resting, and it is important to allow them their dormant period. During this time they need little or no water, so give just sufficient to prevent the pseudobulbs shrivelling. In winter they should also be given as much light as possible to ripen the pseudobulbs.

The resting period may last a few short weeks or several months, depending on the genus. Evergreen orchids which have a brief resting period and retain their foliage from one year to another do not greatly alter their appearance, except that they are flowering during this time. These evergreen orchids include *Cymbidium* and *Odontoglossum*, whose winter care is little changed.

Orchids which have a deciduous resting period are more easily recognized as their foliage is shed in the autumn. These plants should be allowed to dry out and remain dry until the new growth is seen in the spring. These orchids, which include *Lycaste* and *Anguloa*, flower while they are active and starting their new growths.

Many more orchids, such as *Coelogyne*, *Prosthechea* and *Cattleya*, have a long resting period but do not lose their foliage, although the occasional leaf may be shed at any time. Dendrobiums are deciduous, semi-deciduous or evergreen, depending upon the type, and will remain dormant for several months during winter. *Stanhopea* is the exception, most often resting during the summer and starting their new growths in early autumn after flowering, to continue growing throughout the winter.

The very cool-growing *Pleione* and the warmer, deciduous *Calanthe* are among those orchids which have the most complete rest. Their leaves are shed in autumn and they remain completely inactive until the spring starts them into life. To allow total drying out, these orchids may be taken out of their pots and placed in seed trays in full light; they can be removed to a frost-free greenhouse or to a garage, provided there is enough light. Once the shortest day has passed, check them regularly for signs of growth, when they can be potted up for the growing season.

Paphiopedilum and related genera without pseudobulbs have no reserves of water and should therefore not be rested in the same way but kept watered all through the year. They

GROWERS' TIP
Pleione pseudobulbs shed their leaves and remain dormant for the winter. Pot up only when the dormant eye at the base turns green.

require less water in winter, however, as the plants take longer to dry out in response to the lower temperatures and light levels. The monopodial *Phalaenopsis* do not rest for long enough to have water withheld; their cycle alternates between producing a new leaf and a flower spike. A short rest may occur between the leaf maturing and the spike appearing, but watering is maintained at the same rate to keep the plants constantly moist.

Vanda and allied orchids rest from time to time, and this may be during the summer. The aerial roots become inactive as the green growing tip gets covered by white velamen. Lacking pseudobulbs, the plants still need to be kept moist and sprayed to prevent the leaves dehydrating. When the roots send out green growing tips, the plant is growing once again.

Because of the dry atmosphere, orchids resting indoors will need an occasional extra watering throughout the winter, whereas the same plants in the greenhouse will have the benefit of higher humidity. Light overhead spraying on sunny days can also be beneficial, though you should avoid spraying buds and flowers directly. Once you see new growth starting from the base of the previous pseudobulb, resume normal watering and feeding.

Pests and diseases

Orchids growing within a clean indoor environment are unlikely to be bothered by many pests or diseases, but there are a few pests which seem to arrive from nowhere and, if left undetected, can build up into sizeable colonies that are difficult to eradicate. In most cases, there is little need to resort to using chemicals for controlling pests indoors.

The most likely pest is greenfly. These sap-sucking insects can enter the house from open windows in spring and summer and will settle on buds and new growths, causing blemishes on young leaves and deformities on buds. They also excrete a sugary substance which can stick to the leaf and upon which a sooty mould will grow. Where just a few insects are seen, rinse them off in water, using a small paintbrush to dislodge any left behind.

Slugs and snails are a much greater menace in the greenhouse where the humid conditions are ideal for them to breed. They will attack buds and root tips and larger ones will eat into the pseudobulbs, causing a gum-like substance to seep from the wound. Use horticultural sulphur to dry up the damaged part and trap the pest by placing slices of apple on the surface of the compost. Slugs and small snails are attracted to

A leaf affected by bacterial infection.

A leaf showing **Cymbidium** mosaic virus.

Mould on a ***Phalaenopsis*** *flower, caused by damp conditions.*

the leaf with a toothbrush dipped in insecticidal soap. The young move freely around the plant so it may take several efforts to eradicate scales.

Mealybug is up to 3mm (⅛in) long, with a flat, oval shape. It covers its pinkish body with a white mealy substance and sucks sap from the leaf, leaving yellow patches where it has been. Look for this pest in the inaccessible places between leaves and beneath bracts and remove using a cotton bud dipped in insecticidal soap.

Diseases in orchids are usually the result of neglect over a long period, subjecting the plants to stress which makes them vulnerable. The most commonly seen is *Cymbidium* mosaic virus which shows up on the new leaves as a white flecking, which later turns black from fungal infection. The method of transmission is by sap-sucking pests; sadly there is no cure for this virus and any plants you suspect of being infected should be kept away from others until you are sure it is not, or it dies.

The leaves of *Phalaenopsis* and the green pseudobulbs of *Odontoglossum*, *Lycaste* and *Zygopetalum* may be affected by a bacterial disease which appears as a watery blemish and dries up to leave a brown depression. To prevent the infection from spreading, apply sulphur powder to the affected area.

this and will have congregated underneath by the next morning. Other pests you may occasionally encounter include leaf-eating caterpillars and vine weevils. Look out for these and check the plants on a regular basis if damage is seen.

Pests which are harder to detect include red spider mite, scale insects and mealybug. Red spider mite is a minute, reddish-coloured mite which thrives on the undersides of leaves and prefers the drier conditions found in the home. Because it is so small you will usually notice the damage first. This is seen as a silvery white mottling on the leaves, caused where this sap-sucking pest has attacked the leaf. To control, treat all the foliage with an insecticidal soap (available from garden centres in a ready-to-use spray). Do this weekly until the pest and its eggs have gone. The white mottling can turn black as a fungal infection spreads into the dead leaf cells.

Scale insects, up to 3mm (⅛in) long, may be either hard or soft. Adults cover themselves with a white or brown shell and remain in one position on the leaf, moving on only after a yellow patch appears. They can be difficult to dislodge and may have to be scrubbed from

Year-round orchid care

Spring

• Inspect plants daily to ensure they do not go unwatered and give their leaves a daily spray or sponge to keep them fresh and dust-free.

• Watch for emerging flower spikes and mark with a short bamboo cane to prevent accidents where they can easily be broken.

• Support tall flower spikes as they grow, but always leave the flowering part of long sprays free to arch naturally so as not to interfere with the natural position of the blooms.

• Remove faded flowers on the spike before they drop and cut old flower spikes down to the base. Phalaenopsis are the exception; a strong healthy plant can sometimes support a secondary flower spike from a stem. To encourage this, cut the finished spike back to a lower node and further blooms will develop.

• Repot those plants which need it as soon as they have finished flowering. Do not repot orchids with flower spikes unless they urgently need a larger pot and can be simply dropped on without disturbing the roots.

Summer

• For those orchids that can be moved outdoors, find a suitable place alongside a hedge or fence where they will receive early-morning or late-afternoon sun and keep shaded during the hottest part of the day.

• Water outdoor orchids more frequently and increase the feed, as the extra light available will create a harder and faster growth. Hose over the growing area daily to create a moist atmosphere from which the plants will benefit.

• Move indoor orchids to a shadier position for the summer. In hot regions use shade cloth both out of doors and in the greenhouse.

• Make use of humidity trays and spray foliage regularly to ensure orchids are kept cool.

Autumn

• Bring those plants placed outdoors back inside as temperatures start to cool down.

• If orchids are returning to a greenhouse where summer crops have been growing, clean the area thoroughly to remove any potential pests and reduce the chance of infection.

• Clean out the humidity trays of indoor orchids and rinse through the pebbles to remove any algae.

• Where orchids have been returned indoors from outside, they will often lose foliage. If leaves have turned yellow, either allow them to drop off naturally, or cut them off with a sterilized tool where the natural break occurs at the base of the leaf.

Winter

• Damp down orchids kept in the greenhouse less and do not spray overhead as water will stay on foliage for too long. Water only before midday and only on days when the temperature is at least 10 degrees above the night-time temperature.

• Lessen watering for indoor plants but maintain daily light misting or sponging of the leaves so long as the water dries up quickly.

• Place orchids in a light position and make sure they are not standing too close to a window, where cold from the glass could harm them. Drawing the curtains can assist in keeping the cold away.

• Once the shortest day has passed, check for signs of new growth. Where there are signs of active growth, increase watering and give a light application of feed to welcome your orchids into the spring!

Index

Acknowledgements

The authors and publisher would like to thank Sara
Rittershausen as well as all the staff at Burnham Nurseries
for their support in producing this book. They are also
indebted to Dolores Sanchez and to Jasmine Burgess for
their help and involvement in photography. Grateful thanks
are due to Jennifer Vine at the Lindley Library for the time
she generously gave during research into the Royal
Horticultural Society's archive material on orchids.

Photographic acknowledgments

page 21 left Brian Rittershausen; 21 centre © The Natural
History Museum, London; 21 right NHPA/KA Callow; 22
above Oxford Scientific Films/Jim Clare; 22 below Reflex Stock.

Burnham Nurseries

Catalogue and mail-order services are available from
Burnham Nurseries Ltd, Forches Cross, Newton Abbot,
Devon TQ12 6PZ, England, Telephone 01626 352233,
Fax 01626 362167, www.orchids.uk.com. In addition to
offering a wide range of orchids in person or by mail order,
the nursery sells a number of selected orchid collections,
especially for beginners, as well as potting bark and sundries.